COLUMBIA UNIVERSITY LECTURES

LAW AND ITS ADMINISTRATION

BY

HARLAN F. STONE, LL.D.

DEAN OF THE SCHOOL OF LAW
COLUMBIA UNIVERSITY

THE LAWBOOK EXCHANGE, LTD.
UNION, NEW JERSEY
2001

ISBN-13: 978-1-58477-093-0
ISBN-10: 1-58477-093-7

Second printing 2008

The Lawbook Exchange, Ltd.
33 Terminal Avenue
Clark, New Jersey 07066-1321

Please see our website for a selection of our other publications and fine facsimile reprints of classic works of legal history:
www.lawbookexchange.com

Library of Congress Cataloging-in-Publication Data

Stone, Harlan Fiske, 1872-1946.
Law and its administration / by Harlan F. Stone.
p. cm. -- (Columbia University lectures. Hewitt lectures)
Originally published: New York : Columbia University Press, 1915 (Columbia University lectures. Hewitt lectures).
Includes index.
ISBN-13: 978-1-58477-093-0 (cloth : alk. paper)
ISBN-10: 1-58477-093-7 (cloth : alk. paper)
1. Law--United States. 2. Jurisprudence--United States. 3. Justice, Administration of--United States. I. Title.
KF213.S68 2009
349.73--dc22

2008040426

Printed in the United States of America on acid-free paper

COLUMBIA UNIVERSITY LECTURES

LAW AND ITS ADMINISTRATION

BY

HARLAN F. STONE, LL.D.

DEAN OF THE SCHOOL OF LAW
COLUMBIA UNIVERSITY

New York
COLUMBIA UNIVERSITY PRESS
1915

Set up and electrotyped. Published November, 1915.

Norwood Press
J. S. Cushing Co. — Berwick & Smith Co.
Norwood, Mass., U.S.A.

FOREWORD

It was the purpose of these lectures to discuss before a lay audience some of the more fundamental notions which underlie our legal system, and thus by aiding a better understanding and possibly removing some popular misconceptions of law and lawyers to contribute to the cause of good citizenship. The nature of the undertaking precluded any elaborate or technical consideration of the subject, and its thorough and scientific treatment was necessarily sacrificed to the requirements of the popular lecture.

The subject matter of these lectures is familiar to most lawyers and law students. It is not expected, therefore, that professional readers will find originality or novelty, either in their substance or in the manner of their presentation. To the layman it is hoped that they may prove to be of some service in leading to a more just appreciation of the true nature and significance of law, and of the difficulties as well as the importance of its efficient administration.

H. F. S.

CONTENTS

LAW AND ITS ADMINISTRATION

I

NATURE AND FUNCTIONS OF LAW

It has always seemed to me to be a fact requiring some explanation on the part of our educators that the subject of law has received so little attention in our scheme of liberal education in the United States. From birth to death, each of us is subject to rules of law, and even after death the disposition of one's property, the rights of his heirs and next of kin are controlled by law. As citizens and voters, we are called upon to vote upon amendments to our state constitutions, and in many states to vote upon the question whether important legislation shall or shall not be adopted. We elect judges whose duty it is to administer the law in controversies between citizens. We engage in more or less heated discussions of programs for law reform, and all without any systematic or comprehensive knowledge of the nature of law or its origin.

Law lies at the very root of civilization itself, for science, art, commerce, the capacity for coöperative effort by communities and peoples which we identify with civilization, have become possible only through the establishment of social order, which in turn law makes possible, and of which law is the necessary concomitant. The most characteristic feature of all western civilization is perhaps the development of the two great systems of law; the Roman law and the English Common Law, which together constitute the basis of the law of the European continent and of the Americas and are steadily extending their influence throughout the civilized world.

Nevertheless, our educational institutions, while holding fast to the ancient classical learning, and occupying the fields of natural science, economics, and sociology, have with a few notable exceptions left the study of law to be carried on wholly by professional law schools. I would not have the layman receive professional training in law, nor would I have institutions devoted to liberal education give courses in law such as are given in law schools, but there are certain fundamental notions of the nature of law, certain facts relating to its history and development, and certain principles which underlie its efficient administration which should become a part of the intellectual equipment of every intelligent citizen.

It is this belief which has induced me to undertake in these lectures to discuss in as simple and non-technical language as the nature of the subject will admit, some of the essential principles of American law and its administration.

Definitions are difficult and sometimes dangerous to the correct understanding of a subject, yet at the very outset we find ourselves under the necessity of adopting some working definition of law. Many ponderous volumes have been written in the effort to state a theory of law which at the same time should be historically accurate and philosophically sound. Indeed, since law is an essential element in and a product of social organization, any complete definition of law would be impossible without a complete theory of society. It is not strange, therefore, that writers on jurisprudence do not wholly agree on a definition of law and that there are radical differences of opinion as to its fundamental nature. However, our consideration of the subject is not to be speculative, but practical, and our aim must be to find the definition of our subject matter which shall include within its limits all of that material which the lawyer and judge would at once recognize as law and which at the same time will indicate those characteristics which in the eye of the lawyer differentiate law from ethics, morality and social usage, and scientific laws.

Thus viewed, law as it exists in the modern community may be conveniently, although perhaps not comprehensively, defined as the sum total of all those rules of conduct for which there is state sanction. I suppose that we all understand clearly enough what is meant by a rule of conduct, but the phrase "state sanction" is one which perhaps requires some explanation. It involves the idea that the state, which is organized society, will through the agency of government, compel the observance of those rules of conduct which go to make up its laws. Literally speaking, of course, the state does not directly compel observance of law, but it visits certain unpleasant consequences upon those who fail to observe its laws, and thus while it may not compel obedience to law in the particular case in which its aid is sought, nevertheless, by reason of the penalty which it imposes upon the law breaker, its action tends to compel obedience to law in the community as a whole. We speak of the man who eats with his knife, or who fails to raise his hat in greeting a lady, as violating the laws of etiquette or the rules of social conduct, but he has not broken the law, because the state imposes no penalty upon him for his breach of those social rules, whereas the man who steals his neighbor's goods or trespasses on his neighbor's land violates the law, because in the one case the state, acting through the courts, visits upon him the penalty of fine or imprisonment, and in the other it enters a judgment against him for damages for the injury worked by his wrongful act.

It is this notion of state sanction which differentiates the law, in the sense in which we would use it, from the so-called laws of etiquette, from custom and from moral law. By custom we mean the mere habit of action of some body or class of persons. A custom may be commonly accepted and acted upon by the members of the community, but conformity to it is not mandatory so far as the state is concerned. Moral laws may be briefly defined as rules of conduct which are controlling upon us because and only so far as they are founded upon our differentiation of right from wrong. Their origin as well as their sanction is therefore to be found in the moral sense of the community. The law of lawyers or judges is founded essentially upon moral law, although, as I shall take occasion to point out later, there are many rules of law which possess no inherent quality of morality, and they exist only because the safety and order of society require some rule to be adopted, although there is no difference in point of morals, in the several rules, any one of which might be adopted. We shall also see that the lawyer's law does not enforce wholly the moral law, and that there are many rules of morality for which there is no state sanction.

Perhaps, also, a word should be said as to the distinction between law as that term is used by the lawyers, and scientific law, or the so-called laws of nature. By the latter is meant the natural phenomenon of uniformity observed in a variety of ways of the material universe. Stated in simple language, a scientific law is a statement of any manifestation of the universal rule that matter, under like conditions, always acts in the same way. That water freezes at 32 degrees Fahrenheit and boils at 212 degrees Fahrenheit is a natural, or scientific law. That is to say, scientific laws are a convenient statement of the way in which any particular kind of matter will act under given conditions. Natural laws, therefore, unlike lawyers' laws, are not subject to the human will, and cannot be altered by human effort.

Thus we observe at the very outset that law in its essence is made up of those rules of human conduct which are made mandatory by the state upon all its citizens and without which social order and well-being could not exist. Law, therefore, rests on foundations as deep and substantial as society itself. No single element of social organization can be more essential to social welfare than the orderly development and administration of law, and no one assumes a more sacred duty toward mankind than he who undertakes to make and administer its laws.

Since the end of law is the regulation of conduct in the interests of social order and welfare, it is a quality inherent in law that it deals exclusively with the acts of individuals with reference to their relations to others and to things. To use a simple illustration, the rule of social conduct that A shall not assault B is law because the law represented by a policeman will arrest A if he assault B and bring him before a magistrate, who will inflict upon him the penalty of fine or imprisonment because of his breach of the rule which we call law.

The essential fact with which the law is concerned is A's act, which had an effect upon and a direct relation to B, another individual member of the social organization. If A's act were one resulting in an injury to B's automobile, the law would again be concerned with A's act, but in this instance the act is one having a direct effect upon and relation to a thing, and because of his breach of law A might be subject to punishment by the criminal courts, or in an action brought by B against him, be compelled to pay damages for his injury to B's property.

By an act in the legal sense we mean also not only the doing of something by the individual, but in a given case the term may include the omission to do something, which the law, that is the rule of conduct, requires the individual to do. Thus if a city ordinance requires a householder to clear the snow from the sidewalk in front of his house, and he omits to do so, the agents of the law will impose a penalty upon him for his failure to do the precise thing prescribed by law. The failure to do, in this case, is in a broad sense an act, and may therefore be the subject of rules of law.

The term *things,* as I have used it, is not in legal contemplation limited to things capable of physical perception, because it may include all those intangible rights which are capable of use and enjoyment which are recognized and protected by law. Thus the good will of a business, the copyright of a book, the obligation to pay a debt, are all "things" in legal contemplation, although they cannot be weighed or measured by any physical standards. They are, however, rights or privileges, therefore intangible *things* which the law regards as capable of enjoyment, and for the use and enjoyment of which the law makes its rules enforceable by the judgment of courts.

As law is primarily concerned with conduct, which affects in some material and substantial manner the order and well-being of society, through its effect on persons and things, it follows that there are many acts or omissions which fall wholly outside the field of law, because they do not sufficiently affect social well-being to justify their control or regulation by the state. It is for this reason that many acts which are properly considered unethical or immoral or which violate social usage, are not the subject of law. The telling of lies is an immoral act, but the law disregards it unless it is attended by consequences with reference to other individuals or their property of sufficient moment to interfere with the social order. For like reasons habits of dress, the rules of etiquette, and social usage are not ordinarily the subject of legal rules.

As society becomes more highly organized and our moral perceptions become more acute, it is natural and desirable (within limits which I shall hereafter try to point out) that some of the moral or social rules of one generation or epoch shall become the legal rules of the next. Thus, at common law it was a crime to steal and carry away another's goods without his consent, but as late as the reign of George II it was not criminal to obtain another's goods by false pretenses. As was said by the learned justices of the king's court, "Shall we indict one man for making a fool of another," for the law was not for the protection of fools.[1] The time was when a man who ordered goods of a merchant, without expressly promising to pay for them, was not legally bound to pay; or one who circulated false and injurious stories about another was not legally liable for his misconduct. Adultery, although long recognized as immoral, did not become criminal in New York until 1907. Of course these failures of law to realize completely moral standards have, in these particulars, long since been corrected. If time would permit, I would like to trace the successive steps by which the law as in these cases has steadily encroached upon and taken over to itself the field of morals.

There are other reasons why the field of law does not include all conduct or conform completely to the principles of morality or social usage. The law is preeminently a practical system administered by human agencies. The only justification for its existence is the accomplishment of its ends — social order and well-being. Whatever the desirability of a certain result may be, whatever its theoretical excellence, there are practical limits to the extent to which the regulation of human action may be successfully and efficiently

[1] Regina *v.* Jones (1704), 2 Lord Raymond, 1113.

carried. It is undoubtedly desirable that citizens should think only elevated thoughts and indulge in habits which are conducive only to health and morality, but the practical difficulty of regulating the thoughts of individuals and controlling with effectiveness their personal habits beyond a certain limit forbids such matters becoming the subject of legal rules.

It is thus a first principle of law, as it should be of lawmaking, that the law should adopt no rule which in practice cannot be effectively applied, a principle which is too often honored in the breach by our legislative bodies.

Again, in every society there is a point beyond which regulation of conduct ceases to be of social service and becomes burdensome and oppressive to the individual. This necessarily limits the field of law and leaves the control of many human relationships to the individual sense of what is right or desirable conduct.

Another consequence which flows from the fact that law deals with conduct is that it is not concerned primarily with the motives or want of morality of individuals except as those motives or want of morality manifest themselves in acts. Law, therefore, does not inquire into the conscience or concern itself with the moral character of individuals. It is not concerned because John Doe is a bad or immoral man, but it may be concerned if he does a bad or immoral act. The law does not punish an individual because he desires or intends to steal, but if his desire or intention carries him to the point of doing the act of stealing or of doing an act which comes dangerously near to the intended stealing, it punishes him as a criminal. Only in exceptional cases which need not now be considered, does an act otherwise lawful become unlawful or criminal merely because it proceeds from bad motives.

There are certain other qualities which must necessarily characterize law if it is to serve its purpose as means of regulating social conduct. They have characterized the development of all systems of common or unwritten law, and with certain well-defined exceptions they should characterize our statute law. They are, first, that the law should be general and equal in its application, and second, that it should be certain in its application. By a law being general in its application we mean that it should apply indifferently to all members of society under like conditions, or, stated in homelier phrase, the law is and should be no respecter of persons. To have a rule for A which is not the rule for B under like conditions would not only shock our sense of what is just and right, but the rule would lack that universality of application which would be essential to the establishment of social order. There are, of course, many laws, which because of special circumstances involved, apply only to certain classes of persons. A law relating only to physicians or to common carriers would not of course be applicable to druggists or lawyers, but generally speaking, it is essential that they should respectively be applicable to all physicians and to all common carriers, regardless of their wealth or social position or other individual characteristics. In the same way, all citizens should stand equal before the law, and if the citizen is one of the class to which the law is applicable and because of the facts of the case he falls within the mandate of the law, its operation must not be suspended or affected because of either personal favor to or dislike of the individual. The law cannot and does not assume to make all men equal, but it can and should give to the rights of all men equal protection. Only by so doing does it appeal to that sense of fairness or that sense of what is just which must rest at the foundation of all law, and thus promote social order and welfare, which can be promoted only by giving individuals equality before the law, regardless of social status or individual characteristics.

Law must be certain; otherwise its application could not be general and equal. What is law in New York County must be law in Kings County, otherwise a general law applicable to A in New York County would not be applicable to B in Kings County. What has been ascertained and declared to be law to-day must be law to-morrow, otherwise the right which the court enforces for A to-day it may deny to B to-morrow.

In civilized communities, most of the affairs of men are proceeded with on the assumption that the ordinary rules of law applicable to them are known and certain. The business man gives value for another business man's contract, because he knows that the law recognizes the contract as binding and the court will compel its performance or compel the contractor to pay damages for the breach of his contract. A man buys land or a business or a patent right because he knows or can ascertain the law relating to such classes of property and because he believes that the courts will not hereafter change or overturn those rules and thus render worthless his purchase. As civilization becomes more advanced and social organization becomes more complex, the greater becomes the necessity for a system of law, which shall be reasonably certain in its application to the usual affairs of the citizen. Uncertainty in law, when it occurs in the modern state, results necessarily in an inextricable confusion in which loss and injustice to the individual are inevitable consequences. Thus, it is with respect to these qualities of generality, equality, and certainty that we differentiate our system of law from primitive rules of justice or the justice administered by the magistrate sitting in the gates of an oriental city, where the judge administers the law according to his individual sense of what is just and right and without regard to any principle of generality, equality, or certainty.

In the process of discovering the sources of our law it will be necessary to distinguish between what is commonly spoken of as the written law on the one hand and the unwritten law on the other. The common type of written law is legislative law, that is to say, law which is embodied in written form by the action of a duly authorized legislative body. The written statute in such a case is ultimately the authoritative source of the rule of conduct which we call law. When thus enacted it becomes binding on all members of the community to which it is by its terms applicable, and it becomes the duty of the courts to apply it in controversies which come before them for judicial determination. Legislation is thus an important source of written law in this country, where citizens are commonly subject to written laws proceeding from at least three classes of legislative bodies. First, there is the written or statute law enacted by the Congress of the

United States, pursuant to powers conferred upon it by the Constitution of the United States. Typical examples of written law enacted by our Federal legislature are the laws relating to currency and banking, laws relating to interstate and foreign commerce, laws relating to Federal taxes, duties and imposts on importations of merchandise, and laws relating to immigration to the United States. The second source of written law is the legislation of our several state legislatures. Subject to the limitations of the Federal Constitution and of the respective state constitutions, they are authorized to enact statutes having force within the territorial limits of their respective states. Typical examples of written law proceeding from state legislatures are the statutes defining crimes, the statutes imposing liability for causing the wrongful death of another, workmen's compensation acts, the labor law, and of course many others with which most of us are familiar. Finally, in every state the enactment of by-laws or ordinances affecting local government is delegated either by the legislature or by the constitution itself to local governing bodies which may be, according to the system or the territory or community governed, either a board of aldermen, a city council, a city or county commission, or a board of supervisors or select men. Common examples of written laws of this class are traffic regulations, health regulations, building ordinances and other ordinances of a similar character having local application and affecting the health, safety, and morals of individuals of that particular locality. Thus the citizen in any given community in the United States will find himself subject to three classes of legislative or written law. They are the lawful ordinances of the city or town in which he resides and the legislative acts of the legislature of the State in which he resides and of the Congress of the United States.

Not all written law, however, is legislative law. Even in the United States, where there is theoretically a complete separation of the legislative, executive, and judicial powers of government, we nevertheless find the executive, administrative, and even judicial officials promulgating written orders or regulations which are binding rules of conduct recognized and enforced as such by the courts. Under other systems of government than our own we may find legislative powers exercised by the sovereign or by officers of government who are not avowedly legislators, as are the members of our legislative bodies. It will be sufficient, however, for our purpose if we recognize that written law is a rule of conduct reduced to precise written form by any body or official possessing the lawmaking power and duly promulgated as law.

In the United States there is a very considerable body of written law to which the citizens of any given jurisdiction are subject. The Revised Statutes of the United States, which do not include special or private legislation, has now reached five volumes of 5600 printed pages. The consolidated laws of New York, exclusive of all private legislation, in consolidated form, fill ten volumes of over 9800 printed pages, and in addition to these there are of course many local ordinances or by-laws applicable in whatever locality any particular citizen may reside.

Great as is the volume of the written or statute law,

nevertheless it constitutes but a small part of the whole body of rules of conduct which go to make up our law. This brings us to the consideration of the unwritten law.

I think I can best indicate to you what is meant by unwritten law by explaining what takes place when a rule of unwritten law is applied by the courts. Let us suppose that A brings an action against B, claiming damages by reason of B's automobile having collided with A's carriage, seriously damaging it. Let us suppose that the parties are in court and have presented their proof, and that it is the duty of the judge to state to the jury the rules of conduct, fixing the rights and duties of the parties to the litigation. Let us suppose that when the accident occurred, B was driving his automobile on the left-hand side of the street; that A's coachman was driving his carriage in a reckless, careless manner at the time of the accident and that his carelessness was a contributing cause of the accident. The judge would find nothing in the statute law throwing any light on the subject; nevertheless, he would in most jurisdictions state the rules of law governing the case to be as follows:

First: That it is the rule of the road that vehicles should turn to the right in passing and that failure to adhere to this rule would be *prima facie* negligence on the part of the person thus failing and would render him legally responsible for the consequences of his act.

Second: That if at the very time of the accident the negligence of the injured party contributed to it, then he could not recover even if the defendant were negligent, and

Third: Although the plaintiff did not himself carelessly and recklessly drive his carriage, nevertheless he is responsible for the negligence of his servant, the coachman. On the facts as stated, the law is that A could not recover damages for the injury which he had suffered; thus we see that the entire case is disposed of by rules of law which do not exist in any statute or formal written law such as we have defined written law to be. Indeed, the judge in the case we have supposed would probably dispose of the case without resort to any law books, although if in doubt he would find the records of many decisions of other judges who had gone before him where the same rules of law had been acted upon as controlling their decisions.

Rules of law thus declared by judges, which have no existence in the formal enactments of bodies having legislative powers, are spoken of as unwritten law. It is, in short, judge-declared or judge-made law, as distinguished from formally enacted law of legislatures or other bodies or officers exercising legislative powers. But in calling the unwritten law judge-declared or judge-made law it must not be supposed that such law represents the mere whim or caprice of the judge who declares it. Judges are trained in the system of the common law. They recognize the necessity of the principles of generality and certainty in the development of the law and the principle fundamental to the English Common Law that a rule of law once established should be generally followed as a rule of decision in all like cases.

The English common law, which obtains generally

in the United States, is a law of precedent. By this is meant that the decision of a court, when it takes the final form of a judgment, operates not only to dispose of the rights of the parties to the particular litigation pending before it, but it constitutes a precedent to be followed in the decision of all like cases which may arise in the future. Every decision is thus an authority which determines what the law is and is a source of law to govern future cases. Thus we see that judicial decisions are the primary source of the unwritten law and that the judges themselves are its repositories. This statement, however, leaves us still uninformed as to the ultimate sources of the law. Judges decide cases according to precedent, but from whence comes precedent? What is the basis of decision when there is no precedent?

If we go back far enough in the history of the common law we shall find that many rules of law have their origin in the customs of the people, and some in the customs or usages of primitive society. Indeed, some writers, among whom may be included Blackstone, the celebrated commentator on English law, assert that custom is the source of all law. With this we may agree to the extent that law in its beginning was probably the judicial recognition of custom. But on the other hand there are many rules of law which are not directly traceable to or to be identified with any custom. For example, to refer again to our case of the collision between B's automobile and A's carriage. The rule that vehicles in passing should turn to the right is undoubtedly traceable to and founded upon custom. What was habitually done in the community was deemed by the courts to be the proper foundation for the rule of law. The rule that B should be responsible for injuries occasioned by his carelessness is traceable to custom of the primitive community, but the rule that A could not recover for the injury if his own negligence contributed to the accident is not traceable to any custom, and we find it first receiving a judicial sanction in the case of Butterfield *v.* Forester,[1] decided in 1809. The rule also that A should be responsible for his servant's acts probably does not rest upon any custom, and in any event it did not become firmly established until the early part of the nineteenth century. What has actually happened in the development of the law is that from small beginnings originating with custom in the primitive community successive generations of courts have built up our system of common law by gradual additions to it, into a consistent, coherent body of rules and principles. The establishment of a rule based on custom leads ultimately to its elaboration, modification or limitation, according to the new combinations of facts and events to which it may be applied. Once having determined that B is liable for his own negligent or wrongful conduct, it is but a step to the establishment of the rule that he is likewise liable for the wrongful acts of C, which he directs or authorizes, and but another to the rule that he is liable for his servant's acts in the scope of their employment, even though the precise act of the servant is not one which B directed or authorized.

When a new combination of facts is presented for judicial scrutiny, for which there is no precedent, and

[1] 11 East 60.

this is much rarer than is commonly supposed, the court is nevertheless called upon to formulate a rule or rules governing the case. It may be that no case precisely like it has ever occurred, nevertheless it may be found to be within the principle of an earlier case. Thus, if our collision case had taken place between two aëroplanes, we may be reasonably certain that we should find no precedent expressly laying down the law with respect to aëroplane collisions, but the rules establishing a proper standard of care in the case of other classes of vehicles would be some guide in formulating a proper rule for this particular case. It is the duty of the judge, therefore, in formulating a rule of law to govern the case, to find and apply the rule of precedent, if such precedent exists. If there is no precedent existing governing the case, it may nevertheless be possible to extract from the precedents principles which point with certainty to the rule which should be applied. As an aid in formulating the rule resort may and should be had to the writings and opinions of those who have by study and investigation of legal questions become expert in that subject, and finally, the rule when adopted, must be one which will in the light of the facts proved, and of known experience, work well in practice, together with rules already adopted by courts and established as law, and it must also accord with an enlightened sense of morality and public policy. To summarize the matter, the law is what judges having jurisdiction of the case declare it to be. The sources of law are statutes, precedents, custom, the opinion of experts, and public policy tempered and judged in the light of experience.

From the earliest times in the history of English law it has been customary for judges in passing on cases of importance to prepare written opinions giving the reasons for their decisions and referring to the precedents and legal authorities on which they base their conclusions. These constitute the great storehouse of the English common law, and it is only by diligent and prolonged study of them that we become familiar with the principles of law and capable of applying them as lawyers or judges. Since 1292, in the reign of Edward I, these opinions have been gathered and perpetuated in reports of court proceedings. The colonization of the New World was English, or ultimately fell under English domination, so that the English reports furnished precedents for use in the Colonial courts, and afterwards in the state courts, which established the English law as the law of the country. Until comparatively recent times in England the law reports were edited by private individuals, but at the present time the reports of proceedings of the various courts, both in England and in the United States, are official publications, and they include in addition to the opinion of the court a brief record of the proceedings in each case, a statement of the facts in each case, and usually a summary of the briefs or arguments presented by counsel on each side of the controversy.

The reports of the various English courts having jurisdiction in law and in equity now number about 3500 volumes. The reports of the United States Supreme Court now number 235 volumes. The reports of the inferior Federal courts collected in the Federal Reporter now number 210 volumes. The reports in our New

York Court of Appeals number 212 volumes. The reports of our Appellate Division of the Supreme Court number 164 volumes, and the current series of the reports of the inferior courts in New York number 87 volumes. In addition to these there are several series of reports of earlier courts, which were the predecessors of our courts as at present organized, all of which contain more or less authoritative precedents, numbering in all about 315 volumes.

It will be observed from this brief account of the sources of the common law and the methods of ascertaining and applying it, that the administration of law, which rests practically exclusively in the hands of practicing lawyers and judges, requires a highly specialized training, and that the mastery of its history and principles is a work of magnitude.

Do judges make law or do they merely declare law which theoretically already exists and has always existed? Several writers, among whom may be named Blackstone, assert that the latter is the case, and that when a precedent is overruled it is in fact determined that it never was the law. "So that the law and the opinion of the judge are not always convertible terms or one and the same thing, since it sometimes may happen that the judge may mistake the law." This view has often been resorted to to challenge the rather modern argument that after all judges are practically legislators and should make their decisions serve the popular will in very much the same way as the legislative lawmaker. I shall take occasion later to point out that whether we accept or reject Blackstone's view of the function of a judge, his functions are certainly not those of a legislator. Nevertheless the judge does in a certain sense make law. We may test the question whether judges make law by applying the tests of time and space. What was the law of responsibility of the navigator of a steam vessel when Columbus discovered America? What was the rule as to the admissibility in evidence of a telephone conversation at a trial in a court of law in the time of King Henry VIII? In New York, if A writes a letter to B offering to sell him a horse for $100, and B posts a letter accepting the offer, the contract for the sale of the horse becomes complete on the posting of B's letter, even though it is never received by A, but in Massachusetts the rule of law is that B's letter must be actually received by A or no contract comes into existence. If there is an ideal system of law which exists and always has existed for English-speaking people do the decisions of the New York courts represent the law or do Massachusetts decisions represent the law, and have the New York courts mistaken the law? These questions bring home to us in a rather pointed way the absurdity of the assertion that rules of the common law which were unknown and unknowable and which were formulated to meet conditions which the wildest imagination once could not have anticipated, have existed from the very beginning of things.

Undoubtedly these rules were formulated by judges, and when formulated they added something to the law as it had previously existed. This, however, is very different from saying that the rules of law as laid down by the judge represent his whim or caprice. Mr. James C. Carter, the distinguished New York lawyer, in writing on this subject, argued that judges do not make law, but that they "discover law." There is at least verbal inaccuracy in saying that one discovers something which has no existence apart from the mind of the discoverer. We discover natural or scientific laws which exist in the natural universe, even though they be previously unknown. Newton, for example, discovered the law of gravitation, but it is a misuse of language to say literally, for example, that Lord Chancellor Bacon or Lord Coventry discovered the rule that the mortgagor might redeem mortgaged property after his default in paying the mortgage indebtedness. Nevertheless, the term *discover* when used in connection with the process or method by which law is formulated by the just and capable judge has a descriptive quality which commends its use; for example, if the choice of words lay between *discover* and *invent,* I should say unhesitatingly that the former was preferable. The judge, in formulating the rule of law, is guided by the principles of the common law. In determining those principles by the methods which we have described, the duty of the judge should be that of the patient investigator and seeker for scientific truth. To that extent, at any rate, he is a discoverer, and the rule which he *discovers* is a rule which is profoundly influenced, if not controlled, as it is in the great majority of cases, by established principles of law.

In asserting that the judge only discovers preëxisting law, Blackstone and his school are really engaging in the more or less plausible explanation of the fact that judges really declare rules which have an *ex post facto* operation. For example, let us consider the following cases: If A walks across B's land without B's consent, A's act is trespass and he is technically liable to B for at least nominal damages for the trespass. Suppose A passes over and above B's land in an aëroplane. Is A guilty of trespass? There are many statements to be found in the books to the effect that B owns from the center of the earth to the sky. No court, however, has ever decided that an act like A's is trespass and in advance of judicial decision there is no ascertainable rule on the subject; nevertheless, A is subject to the rule, whatever it may be, which may be ascertained and declared by the courts long after his act. It may be in an action which is concerned with the acts of others than A. He may then be held liable for trespass, though no lawyer could have told him with certainty in advance whether his act would be held to be trespass or not. I dwell upon this fact somewhat because it is important that we should understand clearly that unwritten law differs in this respect from legislative law and must necessarily so differ. An act of the legislature does not operate so as to affect cases which have arisen previous to its passage, for it does not exist as a mandatory rule of conduct until duly enacted by the legislative body. We may say therefore that the statute or written law of a given jurisdiction has no rule to govern any particular case if the legislature has passed no law affecting it. This, however, is not and cannot be so of the common law, which because it is the common or universal law must find a rule to govern every case even though the rule was not ascertainable in advance of the litigation by which it was established.

This fact should also be borne in mind in determining the extent to which judges should go in producing violent changes in the common law by overturning established precedent, even when in their individual opinions a changed rule would be beneficial. A change in the rule will affect not only cases which may arise in the future, but all cases which have arisen in the past and which have not been formally adjudicated. The affairs of men, which have been settled and adjusted upon the basis of the earlier and supposedly settled rule, are thrown into confusion, and unjustifiable injury results, by rendering an established rule uncertain or contradictory. This fact demands that the judge should proceed with extreme caution in the overturning or modification of existing rules of law. When change of conditions requires the abandonment of established rules, it is generally wiser and injustice will be avoided if their repeal is effected by legislation which will operate only *in futuro*.

I have spoken of statute law as the written law, but our discussion of the sources of law would not be complete if I did not explain that it is more accurate to refer to statutes as sources of law, for the reason that the scope, purpose, and meaning of every statute must be ascertained by the courts which are the interpreters of statutes as well as of the common law. Every statute is deemed to be an integral part of the whole body of law and must be given a meaning, so far as possible, which will harmonize with the rules of common law not intended to be modified or repealed by the statute. It results, therefore, that statutes, when judicially interpreted, are necessarily given a meaning and effect which they might not have if they were regarded as mere isolated legislative acts. That legislation must be made to work with existing rules of law, not repealed, is a fact too often disregarded or overlooked by our legislators, with the result that many of our legislative acts are a species of legal monstrosity, which if literally interpreted would introduce utter confusion into the law. If given a meaning making it workable with existing law, the courts are sometimes called upon to read into the statute a meaning which practically amounts to a judicial revision of the statute. This is a form of judicial legislation in which courts are naturally and properly reluctant to indulge and of which more will be said in the lecture on law reform.

II

LAW AND JUSTICE

It perhaps may have occurred to you in the course of this discussion that a great deal has been said about law but very little about justice, and the question must naturally have arisen in your mind: Is the law just? What relation has the law to justice and morality? In its last analysis, when we speak of an act, apart from law, as just, we mean that it conforms to that sentiment of fairness which in varying degree is an attribute of the human mind even under the most primitive conditions. We speak of one's act as just or unjust, according as it affects others or their rights or interests in things fairly or unfairly. It is the ethical concept applied to those acts which constitute the subject matter of law which, as we have seen, lays down mandatory rules of conduct affecting men and things. Justice, therefore, constitutes a part of the field of morals or ethics which embraces the whole of human life and conduct, judged according to human standards of right and wrong. We speak of a man who leads a life which does not conform to accepted standards of right as immoral or unethical. When his mode of life leads to acts affecting others unfairly, we speak of them as unjust. The test of justice in the last analysis is the accepted usage or custom of the community, and this, of course, varies in different ages and under different civilizations. Used in this sense, even to the savage mind, it is fair and therefore just that the hunter should be allowed to be possessed of the implements of the chase which he has fashioned, and of the game which he has captured.

As human society becomes more highly organized, the sentiment of justice becomes more fully developed, and takes into account the community interest. We conceive that it is just that the father and head of the family should make sacrifices for the benefit of other and weaker members of the family, and ultimately that the members of the community should yield something of perfect freedom for the benefit of the community as a whole. Thus viewed, every system of law must be founded on justice that is the sentiment of fairness in the community in which it exists, and our primary notion of what is fair or just, in turn, is founded on established usage or custom.

Since law deals with rules of conduct it must necessarily be influenced in its origin and development in ways which will hereinafter be referred to by the sentiment of justice in the community which is our ethical view of conduct so far as it affects others, and it cannot be permanently without the support of such sentiment and continue to exist as a system of law. Turning, however, from the general to the particular, we have all had experiences with the administration of law or heard of cases in which the results have seemed to us crude and imperfect, and therefore unfair. The experience of lawyers is that much of what we hear or read in newspapers of so-called failures of justice is to be distrusted, because it is too often reported incompletely or inaccurately. What appears to be injustice presents quite another aspect when examined in the light of all the facts. Nevertheless, I suppose most lawyers would admit that the enforcement of law may not and sometimes does not lead to results which satisfy our sense of what is fair or just to the individual or to the social interest.

Why is it that law, which has been the subject of solicitous study and devotion through the ages, should be so imperfect as to work injustice even in rare instances? Of course, we must admit at the outset that however just, theoretically, and however wise in system all law may be, it will not reach perfection so long as it is the product of mere human effort administered by mere human agencies. Man is prone to err, and even the just judge, as Blackstone says, may "mistake the law," and juries may allow their better judgment to be overruled by temporary passion and prejudice. The remedy for such failures of justice, like the fault, lies, of course, not primarily in our legal system, but with human nature itself.

Since our whole theory of law is that the individual must sacrifice some freedom of action for the general benefit of the public, it is inevitable that the private sense of what is fair between individuals must to some degree yield to that larger sense of justice which takes into account the welfare of the whole community. The qualities of generality and certainty, to which I have already referred, must necessarily inhere in any general system of law, and may, in any particular instance, affect the application of a rule of law in a way which would seem unfair and unjust if we did not take into account the public welfare. Thus the rule that contracts of certain classes, for example, contracts for the sale of land, must be in writing in order to be enforceable is no doubt a salutary rule based on sound public policy, and may in many cases prevent fraudulent or unjust claims; nevertheless, there are cases where the enforcement of the rule may work hardship and injustice to the individual. The same may be said of the rule that the lawyer or physician or the clergyman may not reveal or testify to confidential communications made to him in his professional capacity, or that an interested party may not testify as to personal transactions with a deceased person in order to assert a claim against the estate of the deceased person. This is true also of the rule of law that a milkman may be convicted and punished for selling adulterated milk, although he had no knowledge of the fact of such adulteration. In all of these cases, and in many others which might be mentioned, the unfairness to individuals must yield to the necessity for a rule having general and certain application, which will protect the community as a whole from certain classes of abuses.

Although the operation of rules of law may be said to be just or unjust in the sense that they are fair or unfair in particular cases, a great number of rules of law do not inherently involve any element of justice or morality. Such rules exist not because there is any question of fairness or unfairness involved, or because it is possible to subject them to any test of fairness or morality, but simply because it is necessary for the convenience of the community that some rules should be adopted and observed. Is it any more just, for example, that vehicles in the street should turn to the right than to the left when meeting other vehicles? yet the law in this country is that they should turn to the right, whereas in England the law is that they should turn to the left. No question of the inherent justice or morality is involved, but it is necessary that some rule should be adopted so that the convenience of the community should be served.

Once a rule of law is adopted, however, it would be unfair and therefore unjust to individuals not to adhere to the rule. Thus, law itself, when once established, expands our notions of justice. Suppose A is induced by B's false statements to sell goods to B under such circumstances that A could, by a legal proceeding, compel B to return them, and that B sells the goods to C, who has no notice of B's fraudulent conduct. May A compel C to return the goods, or should C be allowed to retain them? Both cannot have the goods. One must suffer their loss. Is it more fair or more just, as between A and C, to give the goods to A or to allow C to retain them? Natural justice or the sentiment of fairness offers no solution. Here necessity requires the adoption of some rule which will apply to all similar cases. The rule that C, the innocent purchaser, may retain the goods, has been adopted and adhered to, because, on the whole, courts have believed that it was most convenient in application and most consistent with other rules of law relating to the subject.

Moreover, in determining what is fair or just, the interests of A and C are not alone to be considered, but the community or public interest must be taken into account. Thus there is a public interest in establishing the rule that property offered for sale to innocent purchasers should not be held by the court to be subject to secret claims which the buyer might be quite unable to discover. Many other examples might be given, especially in the law relating to negotiable paper, where the convenience and certainty of business transactions depend upon the adoption of rules which are certain in their application regardless of any theories of natural justice or morality.

Again, a rule or principle of law which does not possess any inherent quality of fairness or unfairness, may nevertheless have those qualities attached to it, according as it is consistent or inconsistent with some other rule of law which the courts have already established. Thus, to recur to our case of the sale of goods. Having once established the principle that C, the innocent purchaser of the goods, procured from A by fraud, may keep them, it would be inconsistent and contradictory to say that C could not sell the goods to any purchaser, even if such a purchaser knew of B's fraud. Having once settled the rule that C is the absolute owner of the property, free from all claims, it would be both unfair, judged by normal human standards, and contradictory to adopt another rule of law depriving C of the benefits of his ownership by limiting the class of purchasers to whom he could sell.

Thus we see that any theory of natural justice or fairness standing by itself will not carry us very far toward the organization of an adequate legal system, and it may be an unsafe test of the sufficiency of any given legal rule. It would certainly be an unwise and unsafe gage of the rights of the parties to a litigation before the courts in a highly organized modern civilization.

When, therefore, we speak of justice in connection with legal matters, we mean justice according to law as formulated and declared by the courts. We do not attempt to judge the rights of litigants upon the basis of any isolated sentiment of natural justice, but we adopt rules of law governing the cases of litigants, and we accept or reject those rules of law as sound only when judged as a part of a system, the aim and object of which is to limit and control individual action and freedom so far only as is needful to serve the community as a whole.

We have already referred to the fact that law deals primarily with the acts of individuals. For obvious reasons it is not and cannot be concerned with the morals or conscience of individuals apart from their acts. This is so because the aim of law is utilitarian. It seeks a definite practical result, namely, the establishment of a rule of conduct which should be capable of enforcement, and one which, when enforced, will contribute to the social order. Courts and juries can weigh and measure human conduct and apply to it legal standards, but it requires something more than finite wisdom to solve the problems of conscience and character. "The thought of man shall not be tried," said Chief Justice Bryan, one of the early English judges, for "the devil himself knoweth not the thought of man." Law, of course, does judge acts according to their moral qualities, but even when law deals with acts with respect to their moral quality, it cannot conform wholly to the moral law.

The boundaries of moral or ethical conduct are necessarily indefinite and shifting. The moral standard of each generation varies somewhat from that of the generation which preceded it. Law, since it establishes a standard to which it demands obedience, must be characterized by definiteness and precision.

It is inevitable, therefore, that law can never realize completely or keep pace wholly with the moral aspirations of mankind, not only because they lack that definiteness along their outer boundaries which must characterize law, but because moral standards must become generally settled and accepted by society before they can find expression in law as an established rule of conduct. The moral rule must be a settled principle of social conduct before the law can or should attempt to make that principle mandatory upon all members of the community.

Moreover the failure of the individual to conform to moral standards, however settled the moral rule and however definite and certain its breach, may not be the subject of law because the social harm resulting from it may not be sufficiently great to warrant the adoption of a legal rule governing the subject. Thus lying, swearing, if not publicly offensive, and other forms of private immorality or unethical conduct, violate the moral but not the legal rule. So far, however, as law relates to acts involving moral qualities, it tends gradually but steadily to conform to the moral standards of the community. Legal history is filled with examples of the gradual expansion of law so as to approximate legal rules to established moral principles. In the early history of the law (Edw. III and IV) self-defense was no excuse for an assault or a homicide. One was legally responsible for killing or injuring another, although his act was the result of a morally excusable accident. In these cases the law took account of the defendant's act only and made him legally responsible for it, regardless of its moral quality, a rule which has long since been swept away in the progress of law toward moral standards. As late as the early seventeenth century one who made false statements about the quality of goods which he offered for sale was not legally responsible to the purchaser unless the seller had expressly warranted their quality; and at a not very much earlier period one who ordered goods or accepted services of another without expressly agreeing to pay a stipulated price for them, was held to be under no legal liability. Such rules did not shock the moral sense of the community when they were established by the courts; but the time ultimately came when the law recognized that one who sold his wares by making false statements committed a legal as well as a moral wrong, and that one who ordered goods of his grocer without asking the price was, nevertheless, legally as well as morally bound to pay a reasonable price for them.

In our own day we have seen the courts in some states establish the rule that a third person may be legally liable for inducing another to break his contract with one with whom he had contracted, or that one may be liable for malicious false statements made of a tradesman's goods, and the indications are that we shall see established the rule that the unauthorized and injurious publication of one's portrait is a violation of legal right. The New York courts, it is true, refused to recognize such a right, but the legislature promptly passed a statute making it unlawful and authorizing the recovery of damages in such cases. In a number of states the courts have held the erection of a spite fence to be a legal wrong, for which the wrong-doer must be held responsible. During the past month the Courts of New York have for the first time adopted the rule that one who procures a contract by misrepresentations even though they be innocently made may not retain the benefit of it. These and many other examples illustrate the capacity of law for self-development, and its constant tendency to adopt moral standards as the measure of legal right.

As we have already seen from our discussion of the sources of the law, the common or unwritten law consists of a collection of rules based upon a body of principles capable of scientific study and classification. These rules for the most part are necessarily artificial in character. By artificial we mean that they do not rest, except in the general sense already alluded to, upon any sentiment of natural justice or fairness, or upon natural law which remains unaffected by human will or action. Law as law, however, must as a whole rest on the belief of the community in its fairness, and it must both serve and maintain the public order and convenience. Thus viewed, too much emphasis cannot be laid upon the fact that law is primarily a product of experience. The necessity that law should be reasonably consistent has already been referred to. A new rule or a new application of an old rule should be consistent with the old; otherwise a citizen who must conform to both rules would be subject to both unfairness and inconvenience. While, therefore, law depends in some degree on logic, its logic must necessarily yield to the test of experience. More comprehensively stated, our proposition is that in the formulation of law the judgment of courts based on experience as to how a given rule of law will work, and of the evil it will remedy, is more potent in determining the rule than either pure logic or theoretical considerations.

The whole system for applying the English common law necessarily leads to this result. No rule of the common law is ever formulated or declared apart from an actual controversy. The facts or events which give rise to the controversy are proved in open court by sworn testimony which is subject to the searching test of cross-examination. The evaluation of fact rests with the jury selected at random from the community at large. The jurymen typify the common experience of the community. The law is applied by a judge who knows the existing rules of law and who by his study of the case and by experience in the practice of his profession and as a judge knows how those rules work in their application to other controversies. If the controversy is one requiring him to formulate a new rule, two questions will be uppermost in his mind. First, is the proposed rule logical or reasonably consistent with existing rules? For inconsistency with them may itself lead to injustice. Second, how will it work in practice? Will it supply the needs of social order and convenience? Will it operate in a way which to the normal mind would seem harsh or unfair? In answering this second question the judge must necessarily draw on his experience and upon his knowledge of the experience of others. If he can meet the requirements of consistency and practical utility he will do so, but if he cannot satisfy both, the rule he adopts must be at least one which will work well in practice.

We live in an epoch of criticism of the expert by the non-expert. Among the criticisms of law and our legal system frequently heard of late is the one that our judges are not competent to administer justice, because they are not sufficiently familiar with "life." What a remarkable ignorance is thus displayed of the circumstances which actually attend the development and administration of law. What phase of human experience is there which does not find its way through the courts? What more complete picture of society as a whole than that to be found in the records of its courts? Assuming that the judge has had the experience and training which should characterize the judge, and if he has not I can assure you that it is not the fault of the law or of the lawyers, but because he is selected by a system which practically ignores the expert opinion of lawyers; assuming that he has had that experience and training, what member of the community has better opportunity to know its life or a larger fund of experience, both personal and the recorded experience of others, from which to draw. Moreover, when a judge declares law, he is controlled not by his untested beliefs, or enthusiasms about social conditions, but by stubborn facts proven in court, and he is sobered by the ever-present realization that by his judgment he is determining the rights of individuals whose case is being litigated before him. It is this which more than any other factor gives to the common law its toughness of fiber, its capacity to resist the abrasion of social and legal theories which do not rest upon the solid foundation of established fact and human experience.

Two impressive consequences of this quality of the common law are borne in on the student who surveys its whole history and development. One is that most of the great developments of common law have come not as the direct result of political agitation or the evolution of legal theories, but because of the steady pressure of facts and events on the courts necessitating the development of new rules which have been formulated in the light of practical experience, rather than as a result of any conscious effort to develop or expand juristic theories.

Thus, while the study of theoretical jurisprudence is an aid to the study and interpretation of law, it has had surprisingly little influence in the actual development and molding of our legal system.

The other fact is that although so largely the product of experience, our laws, so far as they have been ascertained and declared by the courts, will be found, as a whole, when subjected to analysis, to form a remarkably logical and consistent body of rules and principles. It is this fact which makes the study of law by the scientific method so attractive and so necessary if one is adequately to understand and apply it.

Both facts make it necessary that the development and administration of law should be delegated to a learned profession whose chief aim should be first, to ascertain its rules and principles, and secondly, to apply them to the facts, either for the purpose of preventing or avoiding controversy, or for the purpose of securing the judicial determination of controversies which have already arisen.

In all civilized communities having a system of common law there has existed such a learned profession. The experiment tried during the French Revolution, and indeed in our own early colonial history, of administering law without lawyers, speedily resulted in the chaos which must necessarily result from the withdrawal of the administration of law from the hands of those specially trained to administer it. The course of the development of the common law and its ultimate character must necessarily depend upon the integrity and capacity of the legal profession. This subject will be referred to in the lecture on law reform, but from what has already been said as to the sources of law, it must have been apparent to you that the character of law and its administration must depend very largely on the character of the Bar whose members are charged with the administration of law and from whose members its judges are chosen.

Perhaps in no period, and certainly not in the present generation, have law and lawyers been so much the subject of popular discussion and criticism as at the present day. The prevailing social unrest, the impatient desire for speedy, not to say hasty, recognition of scarcely yet formulated theories of social welfare, have found expression in criticism of our whole system of law administration. This public discussion of law and lawyers has resulted in the coining of a new phrase, to which some reference should be made in any discussion of law and justice. The phrase is "social justice."

It has been used in varying senses, perhaps more often as indicating a political theory of social welfare than any other. When thus used as a political war cry, or as the expression of political aspiration, we need have no quarrel with it. Indeed, we are not directly concerned with it in the discussion of law and its administration. But when it is referred to, as it often is, as a principle of judicial decision, we are concerned in ascertaining both its meaning and its application. I surmise that most of the advocates of "social justice" would be puzzled if called upon to define with precision just what idea was intended to be expressed by the phrase. As, however, I read the various discussions of the subject, I gather that two quite distinct ideas are intended to be expressed when it is used as applicable to judicial decisions. One relates to the decision of constitutional questions, when courts are called upon to determine whether or not any given legislative act is constitutional under the 14th Amendment of the Federal Constitution or similar provisions in the state constitutions. Reference will be made to it in the discussion of constitutional limitations. The other, which immediately concerns us, since it relates to the administration of the common law, is the notion that judges, in the administration of common law rules, and especially in formulating new rules of law, should consciously endeavor to mold the rules of law to conform to their own personal notions of what is the correct theory of social organization and development, even though the result should be in many cases to disregard or overturn established rules of law.

As has been stated by a distinguished advocate of

the new principle of social justice as the basis of the so-called sociological jurisprudence, "legal science ought to be founded upon generalizations from a descriptive sociology." As a principle of judicial decision consciously adopted and applied, certainly nothing could be more foreign to the spirit of the common law, and certainly nothing could be more destructive of its essential qualities. Sociological jurisprudence, as thus defined, is really a theory of legislation, since it is an attempt to formulate law on the basis of the legislator's view of what is sound public policy based upon his observation of social conditions, his prediction of what social conditions will be in the future, and his particular theories for improving them.

It is this capacity for adaptation to immediate social needs in accordance with the views of the legislator which gives to legislative law both its weakness and its strength. Even those whose business it is to legislate are not always accurate observers or infallible prophets, and it is the common experience that a large proportion of our legislation proves ineffectual, either because it is based upon inadequate knowledge of the conditions which it is intended to remedy, and attempts to apply impossible or imperfect remedies or because the legislator has not been sufficiently far-sighted to meet all the conditions which may arise in the future. On the other hand, unhampered as it is by the common law, legislation when wisely conceived and skilfully drawn, may effect a prompt remedy for public ills and afford a proper means of limiting or supplementing the natural expression of the common law when the public so wills.

When, however, a judge declares a rule of the common

law he does not legislate. I say this with full appreciation of the fact that judges do create new rules and that they give old rules new applications. As we have already seen, this function of the judge is exercised with comparative rarity. In the vast majority of decided cases the appellate judge is engaged in ascertaining whether established and accepted rules of law have been properly applied to the facts proved at the trial in the court below. It is only on rare occasions that he is called upon to formulate a distinctly new rule of law. When he does this his method and attitude are and should be distinctly different from that of the legislator.

The legislator is concerned primarily with what is good public policy. He is not bound by existing rules of law, and is concerned with them only incidentally in connection with the process of formulating new law, so that the new law may be made effective by clearly repealing the rules of the common law which it is to replace, and by harmonizing with established rules of law with which it is expected to coexist. In determining what is public policy he must necessarily seek to ascertain the opinion of the community, for his mandate to legislate under our system proceeds from the community, of which he is the representative. Moreover, legislation, when adopted, is not the product of the individual mind; it is the resultant of the coöperative effort and deliberation of the legislative body; and finally, legislative law, when enacted, operates only in the future. It can have no application to acts or events occurring before its enactment.

Contrasted with this, the judge's duty is primarily to ascertain whether the facts proved in the case before him are controlled by rules of law which may be found in the precedents. If so, the necessity that common law should be general and certain in its application requires him to apply them regardless of his personal notions of what may be "social justice." If there is no precedent strictly controlling, or "on all fours" with the case before him, as the lawyers say, the principles underlying the precedents may unmistakably point to the rule which should control, and the same considerations would require its adoption. In the rare instances where precedents afford no controlling principle, the judge will naturally consider the opinion of experts as embodied in the writings of those learned in the law. He will consider in the light of experience and established facts what rule will work well in practice, and whether, if adopted, it will conflict with settled custom or usage of the community; and finally, if necessary to the settlement of the question, he will apply his own notion of what is sound public policy.

In determining this last question he is not an interpreter of public sentiment. He need, and indeed ought not to listen with his ear to the ground to ascertain from popular clamor the latest expression of the "newest thing" in social welfare. His function is not political or legislative to enact the popular will or what he may mistakenly believe to be the popular will. His function is judicial, to act as the judge in ascertaining and applying established principles of law when they offer a guide and in accordance with his own conception of right and wrong when there is no other guide.

This is undoubtedly the theory of judicial action as

it has been developed by the English common law. It is based upon the fundamental notion that law must be general and certain in its application, else it is not law at all, but rather judicial caprice on the one hand, or judicial decree controlled by popular clamor on the other.

There is a final and conclusive reason why the judicial formulation of rules of law should proceed on a different principle than the enactment of law by legislation. When the legislature enacts the popular will into law, the enactment speaks only from the day it becomes law. It does not affect any act or event which occurred prior to its enactment. However violent the change of sentiment which may find its expression in legislative action, the new law will not operate harshly on the rights of those whose cases arose before its enactment, and perhaps before the change of sentiment which gave rise to the legislative enactment. The judicial formulation of law has a very different effect. Judicial precedents are *ex post facto* in their operation. The judicial declaration of the law of a case not only conclusively settles that case, but constitutes a precedent for all other like cases, whether they arose before or may rise after that particular decision. That such is the effect of judicially declared law as distinguished from legislative law necessarily results from the nature of a common or unwritten law as distinguished from the written law. The common law must find a rule and make a decision for every case as it arises. As we have already pointed out in theory it declares a rule which is supposed always to have existed. Any other principle would require a court to refuse to adjudicate a case until the rule of law applying to it had been formulated and announced, and would thus do away with the very existence of a common or unwritten law, since common law courts formulate rules only for the settlement of actual controversies pending before them.

Can the judge, therefore, in the decision of a case at common law, found his decision on generalization from descriptive sociology of to-day or upon to-day's popular notion of what is social justice when his decision must not only harmonize with an existing system but must lay down the principle of law controlling the cases which arose last week or last year, or perhaps years ago?

And finally, how is the judge to determine what is social justice? We have seen judges of undoubted learning and integrity violently assailed because their decisions did not meet the views of their assailants as to the requirements of social justice. To the worldly and cynical observer these assaults upon the courts seem not unlike a modern manifestation of the ancient privilege of the unsuccessful litigant to retire to the tavern and revile the court for its decision because from his point of view it was not just. I suppose even our own notions of what is social justice may differ with the individual and, unfortunately for the judge, if he is to base his decision on social justice, not those who cry the loudest always prove ultimately to be right or even to represent the popular will.

I would not be understood as asserting that courts should be always and invariably bound by precedent. There are many examples, of course, where courts have overruled precedents and benefited the law by the process, but I would not have what is normally a rare and exceptional exercise of judicial power cultivated as a habit or resorted to by judges as a method of making effective their individual notions of justice. The power of appellate courts to limit or modify the application of rules of law, and in extreme and exceptional cases to overturn precedents, when wisely and prudently exercised, is the very life of the law. What has led to the overruling of precedent, however, is not the personal theories of the judges as to what constitutes "social justice," but the pressure of facts proven in court which lead ultimately to the recognition that established precedent does not work well, either because it does not harmonize with other earlier rules or because of change of conditions or because it does not square with the settled moral sense of the community.

Even then, if overturning a precedent because of the retroactive effect of the court's decision will overturn settled rights, the court will do well to leave the change of the law to the legislature in order to avoid doing injustice. The power to overturn precedent is one which ought to be exercised with caution, to correct an obvious evil, and never when the wisdom or propriety of the proposed change is open to serious question.

As a philosophy of legislation, our system affords a more or less satisfactory method of ascertaining and applying "social justice." The legislator is elected to his office for a short term, after popular discussion, and usually he stands as a candidate for office on a party platform promising a distinct legislative program. If elected, his election carries with it the mandate of the people to carry out that program. He is thus left in no uncertainty as to the requirements of social justice, and in carrying his legislative program into effect by the enactment of statutes which operate only in the future, he experiences none of the embarrassment which a judge must experience, if he overturns judicial precedents in order to formulate law harmonizing with his theories of social justice.

The judge, although elected in most states, unfortunately so I believe, is not elected to inaugurate or carry out legislative programs. He is, or should be, appointed because of his expert knowledge, experience, and integrity to apply an existing system of law to the settlement of controversies as they arise. That system of law is the accumulated wisdom and experience of our whole civilization, not lightly to be trifled with or overturned. Its history demonstrates that it is capable of progress and expansion, and that it has, in fact, by reason of its own essential qualities, progressed and expanded to meet the reasonable needs of every age. Its progress and expansion has been caused in every instance by the pressure of facts proven in court, and rarely, if ever, by political agitation or by theories of social progress formulated outside the court room. Judicial decisions, according to the common law, therefore justly and properly are a conservative force in the community. They protect the rights of those whose rights may be overlooked or temporarily obscured by popular clamor or in times of political excitement. They are the bulwark of the minority against the tyranny of temporary majorities; of the weak against the strong. As a conservative force, the common law, if it would preserve its character as law, can only follow with cautious and somewhat tardy steps the sentiment of the community, in order that it may not mistake the false and the temporary for the real and the permanent.

Popular error once crystallized into judicial decision produces incalculable injustice, and is exceedingly difficult of correction. Legislation is, or at least may be, the radical force in the community. It responds to the popular will without operating harshly on rights arising out of past events, and is capable of prompt and adequate correction. The common and statute law have supplemented each other in the development of a system of justice suitable to the needs of a free people. Let us not, under the influence of temporary dissatisfaction or disappointment, throw aside the teachings of history and experience by attempting to confuse distinct principles upon which our common and legislative law respectively rest.

III

FUNDAMENTAL LEGAL CONCEPTIONS

HAVING said something of the nature and sources of law, and the relation of law to justice, let us now speak of some of the fundamental notions which characterize our system of law, and then pass on to a consideration of its classification. It will not be our purpose to approach the subject in the same way that a professional law student would approach it, as our object is not to learn how to advise others what their rights are or to undertake as lawyers to protect their rights, but merely to apprehend better of what stuff the law is composed.

We have seen that law, being defined as a rule of conduct with state sanction, relates to the acts or omissions of individuals with respect to other individuals, or to things. Since law is a rule of conduct, affecting individuals, the result of the disobedience of a rule of law is therefore necessarily a particular kind of consequence on some other individual or individuals. The person disobeying the law is subjected to the penalty of the law, because his disobedience has produced a wrongful, and therefore unlawful consequence upon another or others. The person whom the law thus protects from the consequences of unlawful acts is said to have a legal right. In other words, law gives rise to rights in individuals. For example, since the law is that A must not assault B, or trespass on B's land, and since B may apply to the courts to restrain A from violating these rules, or to recover damages for their violation, we say that B has legal rights. We speak of them as the right not to be assaulted and the right to own land and not to have it trespassed upon by one who is not the owner. In substance, a man's legal right is his sphere of freedom of action with respect to others and things as it is fixed and defined by law. We say that law protects a man's rights, meaning thereby that his use and enjoyment of things and the freedom of his person and his character or reputation are protected from anti-social interference and injury by the rules of law which visit certain penalties on those who are guilty of such interference.

It is significant that in most of the continental countries the word of the language of the country which signifies law, and the word which signifies the right of individuals arising out of law, are identical. Thus the Latin *jus*, the German *recht*, the French *droit*, each means law, in the sense in which we have used it. Each also means the legal right of the individual to which law gives rise. In a sense, of course, these terms are equivalent, for the sum total of all individual rights makes up the body of the law, and in turn it is the law which both defines and gives rise to all the rights of the individual.

With us, however, the word "right" is used in a broader sense. We use it not only as expressing our ethical notion of conduct, and as the antithesis of wrong in the ethical sense, but, when used in its technical sense of legal right, it is the antithesis of unlawfulness. It is in this sense that the word is used in relation to the function of courts to redress wrongs. Thus, when we speak of one's right, we mean his right successfully to apply to the courts and set them in motion because some one has done him a wrong, either for the purpose of restraining a violation of law, or recovering damages for its violation; or in the case where the right is to possess property, to have the property turned over to the person entitled to possess it. Thus, all rights, in their last analysis, are rights to apply to some court for its relief, and generally speaking, rights exist only where there is some remedy for their invasion, afforded by some court. If there is no remedy there is no right.

Since rights arise from rules of conduct, every right of an individual has a correlative obligation or duty on the part of some other individual or individuals either to do or refrain from doing some act. Thus, A has a right not to be assaulted; and B in common with other members of the community is under an obligation to refrain from assaulting A. Such an obligation, since it calls upon B to perform no positive act, but merely to refrain from doing an act, might be referred to as a negative obligation, but it is more commonly called a duty. If A sells goods to B, A has a right to collect the purchase price from B, and B is under an obligation to pay the purchase price to A, and since B's obligation is one calling upon him to act, we might refer to it, for convenience, as a positive obligation. It is thus apparent that it is the business of courts to compel in one way or another the observance of legal obligations (including duties) by individuals. Courts do this on the application of one who conceives that he has a right to protect, whom we call the plaintiff, and if he establishes his right, the court compels observance of the obligation by the one obligated, whom we call the defendant. This may be accomplished by directing the defendant specifically to perform the obligation. More frequently, however, the court does not undertake to compel a specific observance of the obligation, but imposes upon the defendant a penalty in the form of money damage for his failure to observe it.

Rights may be conveniently grouped into two classes. One may have a right against all members of the community indifferently. Thus one has the right not to have his person or his property unlawfully interfered with, and this right exists generally against all members of the community. A's right not to have B assault him or trespass on his land is a right which not only exists with respect to B, but against all other members of the community. All so-called rights of property are of this class. One is said to own his house or his automobile against all the world, which means that no one else has the right to interfere with it. Rights of this class are referred to as rights *in rem;* that is, rights in or to the thing.

At common law one could not sue or bring an action against a thing. He could only bring an action against others with reference to it. His rights, therefore, are literally against others with respect to things, and not "in" or " to the thing." On the other hand, one may have a right against a single individual exclusive of all others. Thus, if B owes A money, A's right is exclusively against B, who alone, of all the individuals of the community, owes A the obligation to pay the money. Such a right is known as a right *in personam.* It will be noted that the essential difference between a right *in rem* and a right *in personam* is that a right *in rem* may be enjoyed by the possessor of it without the intervention or aid of any other person, whereas the possessor of a right *in personam* can enjoy his possession or ownership of it only by compelling the obligor to perform the obligation which gives use to the right. Courts, however, act only against designated individuals or legal persons, so that all rights, even rights *in rem,* are protected or enforced by actions brought against individuals or legal persons. Stated in another way, since all rights are enforced only against legal persons, rights *in rem,* as well as rights *in personam,* are protected only by enforcing obligations *in personam.* Thus the owner of land possesses a right *in rem.* The law affords protection to this right only through the medium of a proceeding in the courts, directed against such individuals as have interfered with his right by some breach of legal duty. The right protected is the right *in rem,* but its protection is accomplished by enforcing a right *in personam.*

Several important consequences flow from these fundamental notions of legal right which affect the whole character of English law so far as it is administered by the courts. One is that courts act only when applied to protect or enforce the rights of a plaintiff. All court action, therefore, relates to an actual litigation, the facts of which are proved in open court controversially by sworn testimony, subjected to cross-examination. Court action, therefore, is based upon facts so far as is humanly possible to ascertain and know them, and not upon hasty or imperfect generalizations such as too often characterize sociological investigations where the data are not submitted to the scrutiny and searching tests which characterize the trial of an action at law. This is a fact which should not be lost sight of in judging the responsibility of courts for more or less hesitation in accepting untried social and economic theories and incorporating them into the law.

Another consequence is that the judgments of courts are binding only on the parties who are before the court in any given litigation. This is true even when the right to be enforced or protected is a right *in rem*. In an action brought by A against B for trespass upon land, the court may determine that A is the owner of the land in determining that B had no right to go upon it. This, however, would not preclude the same court from holding that C was the owner of the land in a like action brought by C against A. All that any court assumes to determine by its judgment is that upon the evidence proven before it, the rights of the parties, likewise before it as between themselves, is as the court then determines. Thus it is that although we speak of a right *in rem* as good against all the world, that right can be actually litigated and determined only against such persons as the claimant of the right may make parties to an action to determine it. This must naturally follow from the fact that the courts act only to determine controversies. Therefore they cannot make adjudication of the rights of those who are not parties to the controversy which it assumes to settle.

Another consequence of the established practice that all determinations of law must be controversial, is that when courts are once set in motion, the end sought is the final settlement of the controversy. When, therefore, a trial has been had and the court has pronounced its final judgment, the case is said to be *res adjudicata,* that is, a thing or matter adjudicated, and therefore no longer the subject of judicial controversy, and it is an essential principle of the common law that when the matter becomes *res adjudicata* all the parties to the litigation are bound by the judgment, and they cannot again call it in question as between themselves either in that or any other controversy which may arise. Modern practice is liberal in allowing appeals from judgments, but when those appeals are finally heard and judgment rendered, it operates to put a final end to the controversy which gave rise to the litigation. There are, it is true, ways for securing a new trial on the ground of newly discovered evidence. Applications, however, for new trials on this ground are granted with comparative rarity, and only when it appears that in fact new evidence has been discovered and that substantial injustice will be done if it is not considered by the court.

Having considered the nature of the rights which courts enforce and protect, let us now turn to the classification of law which is commonly made for systematizing its study and better understanding its principles. Law may be classified either with respect to the nature of the right which the courts protect and enforce, or with reference to the character or status of the legal persons whose rights or obligations courts determine. We have already seen that rights are classified according to their nature as rights *in rem* or rights *in personam.* We may now carry this classification a little farther by making a subdivision of these two classes of rights. Rights *in rem* include generally all of those rights commonly spoken of as property rights; that is to say, rights to possess, use, and enjoy things, which rights are good and enforceable against all the world. A man's farm, his house, or his automobile are common forms of property rights, but we have seen from an earlier lecture that one may likewise have property rights in non-material things, as, for example, a patent or a copyright, or the good will of a business, all of which fall within the general classification of rights *in rem.*

But there are a great many rules of law relating to property which bear no direct relation to one's right to recover a judgment for interference with his property. Thus, it is characteristic of practically all rights in property that they are freely transferable from one individual to another; that is to say, it is a legal characteristic of property that it is subject to gift, barter, and inheritance.

The study of the law of rights *in rem* is therefore very largely a study of the rules governing the transfer or acquisition of rights in property. If a man dies without leaving a will, who is entitled to his property? If he leaves a will, what formalities are necessary to make his will valid and effectual? Or, if a man is living, what steps are necessary to transfer ownership of his horse to another by gift or sale? Must there be a delivery of the horse? Must there be a writing? All of these questions and countless others are answered by the law of property, which therefore constitutes a very important and fairly well-defined division of the whole body of our law.

The law of property may be again subdivided into the law of real property and the law of personal property. Real property may be generally characterized as land, and those things so intimately associated with the use of land as to be conveniently subject to the same rules of law as land. Thus, for example, not only land, but buildings affixed to the land, shrubs, fences, a right of way over another's land, are real property.

All property not real property is personal property. Rules of law applicable to personal property are often quite different from the rules applicable to real property under like circumstances. It thus often becomes very important to ascertain whether in a given case property is real or personal. The answer to this question is often difficult, dependent upon a great variety of considerations which need not now be discussed. A few illustrations, however, will suffice to show some of the points of difficulty. A right in land for life is real property. But a leasehold for a term of years, even many times greater than the normal span of human life, is personal property. A key in the stock of a hardware dealer is personal property; but placed in the lock of a door of a house, it may be real property. A field of growing corn is real estate as between the buyer and seller of land, but it may be personal property as between the landlord and the tenant of land. These distinctions doubtless seem curious to the layman, but they are really founded upon sound principles; and the necessity of making them arises from the fact that once having determined that property is real or personal as the case may be, certain important and far-reaching consequences flow from the determination. If, for example, a man dies intestate, leaving real and personal property, his real property goes to his heirs subject to the dower rights of his widow, but his personal property passes to the administrator, to be used by the administrator first in the payment of his debts and then for distribution of the residue among the intestate's next of kin, who may be different persons from the heirs. The proper settlement of his estate will depend, among other things, upon the determination of what part of it is real and what part of it is personal property. The methods of transfer of property also vary widely, according to whether the property is real or personal.

These differences in the rules governing real and personal property are due largely to historical causes. The law of real property is the law of land and of things which, for reasons of convenience, are deemed to be incident to land, and therefore subject to the same rules of law as land. Our law of land originated very largely with the feudal system which William and his successors imposed on England following the Norman Conquest. It was a political and governmental system, founded on the distribution of land of the conquered country in such manner that the recipients of the land subjected themselves and their legal successors to the performance of those services, military and otherwise, which were deemed essential to the maintenance of government. Thus, the whole law of land was so established and developed as to best serve this system. It necessarily differed widely from the law relating to mere chattels, which played no directly important part in the scheme of government. I do not, of course, wish to give you the impression that the law of real property to-day very closely resembles the law of land as it existed between 1066 and the reign of Queen Elizabeth. It has been greatly modified, both by legislation and judicial decision, but most of those characteristics of the law of real property which distinguish it from the law of personal property, and to which we have become so accustomed that they seem to be perfectly natural and desirable, are distinctly traceable to the fact that our law of real property had its beginnings in the law of land of feudal England.

Considerations of convenience, also, led to differences in the rules relating to land and those relating to personal property. The nature of land and methods of dealing with it, on the one hand, and the nature of articles of personal property which are capable of being moved and passed freely from hand to hand on the other, necessarily led to the establishment of different rules of law with respect to the kind of interests or rights which might be created in the two classes of property, and also with respect to methods of transfer of their ownership from one to another.

A great deal of thoughtless criticism of the law in recent times has been based upon the supposed excessive recognition by the courts of so-called "rights of property." Those who have followed this discussion will at once recognize that in this phrase there is an inaccurate use of language which indicates some inaccuracy, not to say looseness, of thought. Property, as such, has no rights. What we loosely call rights of property are rights of individuals against other individuals with reference to things. Property has no existence apart from law, and the great distinction between the lawless or savage community and the civilized community is that in the latter the law recognizes and protects the rights of individuals to the use and enjoyment of things and thus brings the legal conception of property to the use and service of mankind. This conception is as essential and as potent in the protection of the workman's pay envelope as it is to the security of the fortune of the millionaire. Impair the "rights of property" — that is to say, the right of individuals to the lawful use and enjoyment of things — and you strike at one of the great foundations on which civilized society rests. In saying this I do not wish to disparage a proper comparison and weighing of the rights of individuals with respect to things, with their purely personal rights, but to emphasize that the so-called "right of property" is itself nothing but a personal right, the recognition of which marks the beginning of civilization and the transition from the lawless to the lawful community. Even those rights which we regard as individual or personal as distinguished from the "rights of property" are measured in terms of property. If A's rights are interfered with, regardless of their nature, that is, whether they are property rights or mere personal rights, the only relief which a court of law can give him is a judgment that the defendant pay the plaintiff money or deliver to him some other kind of property.

Property, therefore, in legal contemplation, is the standard of value by which man's rights are measured. It may be difficult to say by how much in money or property A's right is impaired when B bruises A's face by an assault; but no other standard of measurement has been devised. If the standard is deprived of its attributes, the right itself, regardless of whether it be a right of property or not, loses some measure of the protection afforded to it by the law. By this I do not mean to say that the law may not properly regulate or limit the use of property, according to whether or not its use interferes with social order and well-being. A great deal of the substance of law relates to just such regulation and limitation of the lawful use of property. But a point I would emphasize is that in the last analysis there is no such thing as rights of property as distinguished from the rights of man, and that, therefore, courts and legislatures cannot impair the right of use and enjoyment of things without ultimately producing some interference with the rights of men in relation one with another.

Having thus classified rights *in rem*, or property rights, some attention should now be given to the classification of rights *in personam*. Rights *in personam*, as we have seen, are rights against a limited number of specified individuals, and in the event that these individuals fail or neglect to perform their legal obligations, the corresponding right can be enforced only by resorting to the courts. They are, therefore, rights of action, or as they are sometimes called, things or *choses* in action; things, because the law recognizes them as capable of use or enjoyment and therefore subject to legal rules of conduct governing individuals with reference to them. Rights *in personam* may be conveniently classified into rights in contract, rights in tort, and rights in what the modern law writers have termed "quasi contract."

By the term "rights in contract" we mean all those rights to recover from a defendant because he has failed to perform a promise made by him to the plaintiff, which the law regards as obligatory. The obligation in contract differs from other legal obligations, in that it is imposed upon and enforced against a defendant because originally he intended to assume it, whereas most legal obligations are imposed regardless of the intention of the defendant, and usually in spite of his intention. Obviously there are many promises which are not legally obligatory, because they are not intended to become such. A promise to attend a dinner or to keep other social engagements is not a contract, for one reason, among others, that the circumstances are such that the parties clearly understand that no legal obligation is intended to be entered into. Examples might be multiplied of purely social obligations which, however, are not legal because not intended by the parties to the transaction to be such.

When, however, there is the intention to enter into a contract, and by intention we do not mean the secret intention of the defendant, but his intention, judged by external standards and manifested by his conduct or by written or spoken language, then he may be legally bound if the other requisites of a contract are present. The intention to be bound must result in a promise on the part of the defendant, which may be expressed in language written or spoken, or it may be inferred from his conduct and it must be accepted by the plaintiff. If A gives an order to his grocer for the purchase of goods to be delivered, and the grocer accepts the order and fills it, the law finds no difficulty in inferring that A has promised to pay for the goods, although there is no promise expressed in written or spoken words. The grocer understands that A, by his conduct, holds himself out as undertaking to pay for his purchase, and this, undoubtedly, is the fair interpretation to be placed on A's acts, judged in the light of common experience.

According to the English common law, contracts may be classified as simple contracts and contracts under seal. The former includes all those contracts which may be valid, regardless of their form; that is, regardless of whether they are in written or spoken language or inferred from the conduct of the parties. Contracts under seal are contracts in which the promisor's promise is expressed in a writing, to which the promisor has affixed his seal. Such contracts were at common law valid and enforceable if the promisor went through the formality of affixing his seal and delivering the document to the promisee or some one for him, regardless of whether any consideration was given by the promisee for the promisor's promise. Sealed contracts are still valid and enforceable, subject to certain limitations which need not here be referred to. The law of the subject is an interesting survival from the age when the creation of legal rights depended on the form or ceremony with which the transaction was effected.

Another distinction between contracts under seal and simple contracts was that the validity of the latter always depended and still depends upon some consideration being given by the promisee for the promisor's promise. The consideration may be and usually is money or property given to the promisee by the promisor; but it may also be the giving up or surrender of any right possessed by the promisee, even though it benefit third persons rather than the promisor, if the surrender is made in return for the promisor's promise. Thus, if A owes B, and C promises to pay the debt if B will release A, and B does so, a new contract arises between B and C, C having given his promise for consideration, namely, the release of A by B. In the same way a contract may arise by an exchange of promises, each promise being consideration for the other. Thus, if A promises to sell a horse to B and B agrees to purchase that horse at an agreed price, a good contract would come into existence by the mere exchange of promises. The rule that simple contracts must be founded upon consideration goes back to the antiquity of the law and its origin is due to purely historical reasons, but it has been perpetuated by the law because it is a principle essentially sound and just that one should not be legally bound by his promises unless he receives something in the nature of a consideration for his promise.

It is a principle of the law of contracts that the parties to the contract must reach an agreement or meeting of the minds as to all the terms of the contract, if they are to be bound by it. Thus, if A, in offering to enter into a contract, by mistake offers something different from what he intends to offer, and B knows of the mistake, he cannot create a contract by accepting the offer, for there is not a complete agreement of the two minds of the two parties to the contract as to all of its terms. There are, of course, many other rules governing the formation and discharge of contracts of great importance to the lawyer and the law student, but which cannot be touched upon in a brief discussion of the subject. The important consideration for our purposes is that rights and obligations in contract are acquired and incurred as a result of the voluntary act of the parties, and the whole law of the subject rests upon the principle that social welfare is guarded and promoted by rendering obligatory the promises of individuals entered into under proper conditions.

Rights in tort arise from breaches of legal duty other than those of contract. The word *tort,* which came into the language from the Norman-French, means literally wrong. The plaintiff's right in tort is therefore a right which arises from the defendant's wrong-doing or in his failure to do something which the rules of law require him to do, which act or omission has resulted in injury to plaintiff. We have already referred to those rights which the possessor of them may assert against all the world, including those personal rights and property rights which the law protects from interference by others. While we speak of these personal rights or these rights *in rem,* or property rights as rights good against all the world, nevertheless, owing to the fact that rights are protected only by action of the courts, and since courts act only to settle controversies between individuals, such rights can be judicially protected and enforced only by entering judgment against the particular person or persons who interfere with the plaintiff's rights.

Thus personal rights and property rights good against all the world when interfered with give rise to rights *in personam*, which, for lack of a better generic term, we call torts or wrongs. To illustrate, if A, the owner of land, has a right, good against all the world, which we call a right *in rem*, the courts can act to protect that right only when it is interfered with by some individual whose act is a tort or wrong for which he is legally bound to pay damages. There is no contract, for he has not promised not to trespass. His legal obligation or duty not to trespass is not self-imposed, but is imposed on him in common with all other members of the community. A's right arises from the breach of this legal duty not to interfere with A's property. Torts, therefore, are all those rights *in personam* to recover damages for unlawful interference with those personal and property rights which we have referred to as rights good against all the world.

The simplest illustration is the case of wrongful taking of personal property, or assault upon the person. In the one case the defendant is under a legal duty not to take the plaintiff's property and in the other not to assault him, because the common law, as interpreted by judges, has definitely established these rules of conduct. If the defendant violates these rules he commits a legal wrong, or tort. It is for the court, aided by a jury, to decide what will be the loss or damage suffered by the plaintiff by reason of the defendant's wrong.

Other forms of tort which may be mentioned are slander and libel, which are respectively the malicious speaking or writing of another, tending to bring him into contempt or subject him to ridicule; deceit, which is knowingly making a false statement to another, for the purpose of inducing him to do or not to do a particular thing, to his damage; and malicious prosecution, which is the malicious prosecution of another for crime without reasonable cause.

A very considerable portion of the law of tort is the so-called law of negligence. It is a recognition of the principle that in the civilized community men must so act and so conduct their affairs that they do not cause unnecessary or unreasonable annoyance or injury to others. The standard of conduct which the law has set up is that of the reasonable man exercising reasonable care and prudence. If one so acting causes injury to another, he is generally not liable in tort for his acts. If, however, his conduct has been negligent, if a common law jury finds that the injury was the result of the defendant's failure to act the part of the reasonably prudent man, then the defendant is liable in tort for his injuries.

To this principle must be added another, namely, that one is liable for the negligent acts or omissions of his servants while they act within the scope of their employment. Philosophically, it has always seemed to me extremely difficult to explain or justify this rule. If one uses due care in the selection of his employees, provides them with proper implements, makes proper rules and regulations governing their employment, in short, if the master has in all particulars acted the part of the reasonable man, how can he be said to have failed in any duty because his employee has been negligent and thus injured a third person? At best, it can be said to be only a convenient way of imposing on a trade or business the cost of the injuries which may be incidental to it. The difficulty with the rule from this viewpoint is that it is not limited to employees in trade or business, or to injuries which in any proper sense may be said to be incidental to them.

Liability for negligence is subject to three common law limitations known as the contributory negligence rule, the assumption of risk rule, and the fellow-servant rule. By the first is meant that one may not recover for injuries if at the very time of the accident or injury the plaintiff was himself guilty of negligence which contributed to the accident or injury. By assumption of risk is meant that if a plaintiff knowingly does an act under such conditions that it involves risk of injury to himself, then he may not recover for injuries resulting from that risk, even though they were contributed to by the defendant's negligence. By the fellow-servant rule is meant that in the employment of a fellow-servant by an employer under such conditions that the negligence of one servant would naturally result in the injury of another or other servants, the injured servant or employee cannot recover from the employer for such injury.

Much of the current discussion of the subject in connection with various phases of workmen's compensation has proceeded as though those rules were ingenious inventions, devised for the purpose of imposing hardship and injustice on the working-man, and that their adoption was purely the result of class selfishness. As a matter of fact, the contributory negligence rule and the assumption of risk rule originated in cases not involving employees, and have always been generally applicable to all plaintiffs in tort cases, whether they were employees or not. There is nothing very shocking to our sense of fairness or inconsistent with the orderly conduct of life in holding that one who has freedom of action and who contributes to an accident by his own negligence, or who deliberately runs the risk of an injury from an apparent danger, should bear the consequences of his folly. The fellow-servant rule was a not unnatural limitation upon the rule that an employer is absolutely liable for his servant's negligent acts, regardless of the employer's own care and prudence, a rule, the arbitrary and unphilosophical character of which has already been referred to.

A careful consideration of the history of the subject will convince the impartial critic that these rules of law are not in any sense due to class selfishness, nor did they at the time of their origin operate harshly or unjustly, or contrary to sound public policy. Nevertheless, the tremendous industrial changes which have taken place in the last generation, and the rapidity with which they have been brought about, have created a situation such that the rules to which we have referred limiting the right to recover in negligence cases, operate harshly in the case of employees in large industrial enterprises. In the case of large industries we have come to realize, especially in the case of dangerous trades and callings, that there is a pretty definite amount of injury to workmen and consequent loss which economically should not fall upon the employee in the trade, but should be added to the cost of production, and if under existing rules of law there is legal liability on the part of the employer, our method of establishing it and imposing the burden on him is economically wasteful. The assumption of risk rule has seemed especially harsh under modern industrial conditions, since it cannot fairly be said that the industrial employee is free not to assume the risk of his employment or that he stands on a plane of equality with the employer in entering into the contract of employment.

Changes of condition so extensive could only be adequately and promptly met by comprehensive legal changes necessarily worked out by legislation. This is being accomplished by the adoption in many states of the so-called workmen's compensation acts, the aim of which is threefold. The ends sought are, first, the abolition of the assumption of risk rule, the contributory negligence rule, and the fellow-servant rule in all cases of injuries to employees injured in the course of their employment; second, the imposition on the employer in certain classes of industries of the cost of injuries to employees as a part of the cost of production in those industries, by making the employer absolutely liable for injury to his employees, regardless of his own negligence; and third, the avoidance of the present wasteful methods of imposing liability on the employer, by establishing a fixed scale of compensation for injuries, so as to minimize the chance of controversy requiring judicial determination. Incidentally, it is the aim of all workmen's compensation acts to effect a distribution of the cost of workmen's compensation over the industry affected by it. This is accomplished by requiring the employer to take out insurance against loss incurred through the operation of the workmen's compensation acts. This may be effected through the medium of state insurance, as is done in Germany and England, a plan which has been adopted in part in New York, or by effecting insurance with private insurance companies, as is more generally done in the United States.

Even with the aid of a constitutional amendment and with the exercise of unlimited legislative power, the solution of this problem is not simple. It is undoubtedly economically desirable, but the economic value will depend very largely upon the care and skill with which the scheme for compensation is incorporated into legislation, and the fidelity with which public officials carry it into effect.

But a word need be said about rights and obligations in quasi-contract. The phrase means an obligation like — or as if — upon contract. That is to say, there is a certain class of obligations where the defendant is legally obligated to pay money, although he has entered into no contract and he has been guilty of no breach of duty rendering him liable in tort. For example, the obligation to pay a judgment obtained by a plaintiff against a defendant is quasi-contractual. The obligation to pay a statutory penalty is quasi-contractual. The obligation of a defendant to repay money paid to him by mistake is quasi-contractual. The defendant having received the money innocently and not having promised to pay it back is neither guilty of tort nor breach of contract, although he is legally obligated to pay the money. In short, all those obligations which arise when a defendant is under legal duty to pay or return money, outside of any duty in contract or tort, are grouped together as obligations in quasi-contract.

Historically, the obligation to pay money received from another by mistake, or to repay money or money's worth, to prevent unjust enrichment by a defendant at the expense of the plaintiff, which constitutes a large part of the law of quasi-contracts, is a much later development than either contracts or tort. Its adoption and gradual expansion by the courts illustrates, perhaps more than any other branch of law, the tendency of law to make moral standards legal standards, and thus gradually occupy the field of morals.

Rights *in personam*, or rights of action in contract, tort, and quasi-contract, were regarded by the early common law as purely personal in character, and therefore could not be transferred from one person to another, as was the case generally with rights *in rem* or property rights. An exception to this rule was the law of negotiable paper, that is, promissory notes, checks, and bills of exchange. By the custom of merchants, the contracts represented by these instruments were freely transferable by endorsement, just as they are to-day, and the custom of merchants with respect to these instruments was adopted by the common law.

This was not true, however, in the early law in the case of ordinary contracts or of claims in tort or *quasi-contract.* Modern statutes now permit the transfer by assignment, of contracts and of some claims in tort arising out of injuries to property, and of quasi-contracts, so that to this extent rights *in personam* resemble rights *in rem*, and thus, to a limited extent, rights *in personam*, which are freely transferable, give rise to rights *in rem*.

IV

FUNDAMENTAL LEGAL CONCEPTIONS

(*Continued*)

We have seen that law may be conveniently classified according to the nature of the rights which it creates. In thus classifying law we speak of the rights and the corresponding obligations of normal legal persons. These rights, however, may vary in their character and require a further classification according to the character of the person possessing such rights, or subject to corresponding obligations. For example, when we deal with the law of contracts we deal ordinarily with the law as applied to the ordinary person of full age and normal legal status. Rights and obligations in contract, however, may be very different if the persons concerned are infants, married women, insane persons, or corporations, since each of these legal persons does not possess the same rights nor are they subject to the same obligations in all respects as normal legal persons. Thus, a practical working classification of legal rights — and thus of the whole field of private law — could be represented in a diagram somewhat as follows:

PRIVATE LEGAL RIGHTS

	NORMAL LEGAL PERSONS	INFANTS	MARRIED WOMEN	INSANE PERSONS AND INCOMPETENTS	CORPORATIONS
Property					
Contracts . . .					
Torts					
Quasi-contracts .					

If a lawyer were called upon to determine the legal rights of any given individual or wished to consult the literature of the subject, he would endeavor unconsciously, perhaps, to so direct his inquiry as to bring it within the limited field of the law represented by one of the squares indicated on the foregoing diagram. He would first ascertain whether the right involved were one of property, tort, contract, or quasi-contract. Having ascertained that fact, he would next have to ascertain the status of the individual whose rights were the subject of inquiry; that is, whether the individual was a normal person of full age, an infant, — that is, a person under twenty-one years of age — a married woman, an insane or incompetent person, or a corporation. The square formed by the intersection of the respective areas assigned to the two kinds of legal rights to which the selected individual is subject, would thus represent and include the law applicable to the particular individual.

The classification of rights according to the nature of persons possessing them is much simpler under the English Common Law than it may be under other legal systems. The Roman law, for example, recognized many kinds of status which were never recognized under the English Common law. Thus, under the early Roman law one's rights might not only vary according as that one was an infant or a married woman, but they might depend on the answer to the question whether he was free or a slave, or whether a freed man or a Roman citizen, or whether a Roman citizen or a foreigner.

Infants, that is to say, persons under twenty-one years of age, because of their tender years and want of maturity of mind, are generally not subject to the same rules of law as adults. Generally speaking, an infant may own or acquire property. He is liable for his torts and in quasi-contract, but he is not absolutely bound by his contracts, which may be avoided by him on his coming of age or for a reasonable time thereafter. There are various other legal relations in which the fact that the person affected is under the age of twenty-one may be of importance. Thus, infants under twenty-one may not make wills of real estate in most states and under eighteen they may not make wills of personal property. Parents exercise certain rights or control over their children until they reach their majority, and are entitled within certain limits to have their wishes with regard to their child's education and maintenance respected, and on the other hand may be compelled to supply their children with necessaries and reasonable support. The term "necessaries" is somewhat elastic, but it is deemed to include all those articles and services reasonably required for the support, maintenance, and education of the child, having in mind his social position and the financial means of the parent. If the parent fails to provide these, any person so providing them may recover their reasonable value from the parent.

An infant is not under the same responsibility as an adult for his criminal acts. At common law, infants under seven years of age were regarded as not capable of committing crimes. Between the ages of seven and fourteen there was the presumption that they did not have sufficient knowledge of right and wrong to be guilty of crime, a presumption, however, which might be rebutted by proof offered on behalf of the state. In many states, as in New York, the period during which this presumption operates has been reduced to the period from seven to twelve years. These and numerous other examples which might be given, suffice to illustrate the principle that rules of law as established for normal persons may vary widely, according to the special status of the person affected by them.

Unmarried women at common law possessed the same rights as men except with respect to the right to inherit real estate. Under the English law of primogeniture male heirs were preferred to female, but if there were no male heirs, female heirs within the same degree of relationship to the ancestor shared in his real estate equally. Under the statutes of inheritance generally in force in the United States the rule of primogeniture does not exist and sisters inherit real estate equally with their brothers.

Under the common law when a woman married it was practically true for most purposes that the husband and wife were legally one and that he was the one. At common law he was the legal head of the family; by marriage he acquired the right to the wife's services and to all her personal property except articles of dress and personal adornment. He acquired the right to use her real estate during their joint lives, and if children were born of the marriage, he acquired the right to use it during his own life and after the wife's death. By marriage she lost completely the power to contract; she could not sue or be sued apart from the husband, but she might acquire property subject to the husband's rights. In consequence of the husband's rights he was liable for the wife's torts and for her contracts existing at the time of her marriage. On the other hand, the wife had an absolute and indefeasible right to dower, which was a one-third interest for life in all the husband's real estate.

These rules of law were of course a product of social conditions peculiar to a bygone age, and have long since been changed by legislation. Beginning about the year 1848, both in England and the United States, a series of legislative acts were passed, giving to married women a measure of legal independence and increasing their rights of enjoyment and control over their own property. The scope of this legislation has been gradually broadened until at the present time in the state of New York, for example, married women enjoy, if they assert their rights, practically the same rights with respect to their property as men. Indeed, the law gives to a married woman some advantages with respect to her property over those enjoyed by married men. For example, a married woman's right to dower in the real property of the husband remains unimpaired, whereas the husband's right to enjoy the use of real property of the wife after her death may be cut off by the wife's will or by her conveyance of her real estate in her lifetime. Under the statute in New York, married women are entitled to their own earnings if they claim them, and they may contract freely with their husbands or with third persons.

Corporations are, in legal contemplation, legal persons possessing rights and being subject to obligations, but their rights and obligations differ in various particulars from those of the normal legal individual. In a sense, of course, the corporation as a legal person is a fiction. What happens when a corporation is organized and acquires legal rights and becomes subject to legal obligations is that a number of individuals are permitted, by following the rules prescribed by the legislature, to associate themselves together for the purpose of conducting business as a corporation. They become entitled to use the corporate name, to sue and be sued in that name, to acquire property and rights, and to be subject to obligations. A peculiarity of the transaction is, however, that the corporation and not the individual members is deemed to acquire the rights and to be subject to the obligations. The corporation is thus a legal entity possessing to a limited degree only, the rights of individuals. These rights correspond to the rights of individuals only so far as the statutes and courts give to the corporation the attributes of a legal person.

There is a common belief that the corporations are the favorites of the law and that they possess legal rights and advantages not possessed by ordinary individuals.

Quite the opposite is the fact. No corporations possess all the rights of the normal individual. They are not afforded the same legal protection or the same immunities legal and constitutional as are normal individuals, and in practically all states they are subject to statutory requirements with respect to taxation, in the matter of filing reports in various public offices, and in subjecting their business and affairs to inspection and investigation of public officials, which are not required of private individuals.

The legal advantage of doing business in the corporate form results from the fact that the owners of the corporation, who are its stockholders, are in most states not legally liable for the debts of the corporation and only the property belonging to the corporation, as distinguished from its stockholders, may be taken for its debts. Another advantage is that the individual or individuals controlling a majority of its stock may within certain limits control the business and affairs of the entire corporation. The other advantages are economic and not legal. It is through the medium of the corporation that it has been possible to bring about coöperative effort in the great business enterprises which have characterized the economic development of the nineteenth century. On the other hand, the ability of limited groups of individuals to control great aggregations of capital through the stock control of corporations has given rise to most of the serious economic problems growing out of the modern growth and development of business corporations.

The power of corporations to contract and to acquire and dispose of property depends upon the powers conferred upon it by its charter or other instrument under which it is created. As a corporation is impersonal, it can only act through its officers or agents, but corporations are now generally held to be liable for their agents' torts, regardless of their nature, committed in the course of their agency, and the tendency is to hold corporations liable for the crimes of their agents in like manner, although obviously the only penalty which can be imposed on the corporation for its crimes is a fine, or its dissolution.

A very considerable part of the law of corporations deals with the rights and obligations of the corporation with respect to its members, that is to say, the corporation not only may have rights and be subject to obligations with respect to third persons, but there are many rules of law relating to the control of the corporation by its members, their rights to share in the conduct of its business and the profit earned by that business, all of which taken together go to make up the great body of corporation law.

A further classification of law with respect to the nature of the legal person whose rights are being asserted is the division of law into public and private law. By private law is meant that body of rules which relates to the normal private individual. By public law is meant all that body of rules of law which relate to and directly affect the commonwealth, which, organized as a corporate body, is deemed possessed of rights and is therefore a legal person.

It would, of course, be inaccurate to say that this is the only difference between public and private law. Public law is public law not only because it affects the commonwealth in the form of the state or some corporate political division of it, but because the character of the rights relating to such legal persons is influenced by the fact that a public legal person rather than a private individual is affected. That is to say, a difference in the legal person whose rights are being asserted according as it is a private individual or the commonwealth, produces a difference in the character of the rights themselves. Again, law, whether public or private, cannot be said to exist wholly for the state or wholly for the individual. Private law is affected by the fact that it has a relation to the public as a whole and public law is affected by the fact that it frequently has application to private individuals. We may say, however, that public law in the first instance relates to and serves public interests, whereas private law relates to and serves in the first instance the rights of private individuals.

An important branch of public law is international law, or the law of nations which embraces those rules of conduct regulating the intercourse of nations and fixing their rights with respect to each other and the relations of each with the citizens of the other. Many of these relations are, of course, regulated by treaties, voluntarily entered into by nations. The procedure for enacting treaties, their interpretation, the remedies for violation of treaties, are all questions of international law. International law, however, includes rules of conduct as between nations and their respective citizens, even in cases where they are not regulated or governed by treaty. The law of citizenship, the rights of belligerents and neutrals in time of war, the law of contraband, the law of prize, are common illustrations of international law.

Many writers have denied to international law the character of law, because in a narrow sense it lacks sanction; that is, any organized coercive force other than public opinion is wanting to make its rules obligatory. While it is true that there is no universal tribunal to which all questions of international law may be brought for judicial determination, there are, nevertheless, a great many agencies created by treaty or coöperative effort of governments which tend to give to the rules of international law more than mere moral force. The various international conferences at which rules of conduct have become the subject of discussion and agreement more or less informal, the Hague conferences, the informal mutual support of each nation by others in maintaining generally accepted principles of international conduct, while not formally amounting to sanction in a technical sense, have nevertheless given rise to the general recognition of certain rules of conduct as established, so that a nation through its foreign office is regarded as justified in relying upon the existence and general recognition of such rules and enforcing them by the use of its armed forces.

Moreover, the rules of international law have not infrequently become the subject of inquiry by courts in order to determine the rights of litigants, in which case, of course, the rules of international law are ascertained and applied by the courts in the same way as rules of private law, and international law thus has to that extent a complete and formal sanction. Our own Federal courts, for example, have been called upon at various times to interpret treaties, to determine in a given case whether a state of war existed, whether a blockade existed, what was lawful prize and contraband, the rights of neutrals and belligerents, and many other questions of purely international law.

The English prize courts at the present time, in passing upon prize cases, are required to pass upon like questions. In so doing they are applying definite rules of law for which there is a definite sanction. Thus, for all practical purposes, we may consider international law under these circumstances as having most of the attributes of formal law.

Each great national or international conflict of the past has tended to settle doubtful or disputed questions of international law, and thus increase the area of regulated international action. The tendency has been toward the strict observance of the rights of neutrals and to minimize the harsh consequences of war to non-combatants. The immediate consequence of the present war has been to reverse this tendency, and rights of neutrals and of non-combatants which it was believed were at least recognized as valid by common consent of the civilized world have been repeatedly disregarded by belligerents during the present war. The steady expansion of the doctrine of continuous voyage, the bombardment from airships of non-fortified towns and cities by operations not involving any military purpose, the levying of enormous fines on captured municipalities, the devastation of whole cities for alleged infractions of military rule, the laying of mines on the high seas, the sinking of merchant vessels, both neutral and belligerent without search or warning and without removing their passengers and crews, are examples of the wholesale sweeping away of the principles of international law, which is one of the regrettable results of the present terrible conflict. The progress made in international law in the one hundred years since the Napoleonic wars has for the time being been lost, and at the present time rules relating to neutrals and non-combatants seem more like pious hopes or aspirations than legal rules.

Nevertheless, it is historically true that the greatest progress in international law has come about through the influence of public opinion aroused by the overriding of those principles of morality and justice which have gradually won their acceptance by enlightened nations as the proper basis for rules governing international relations. One of the fortunate consequences which it may be hoped will result from the present war is the more complete acceptance of those rules of international law which tend to mitigate the savagery of war in its effect on both belligerents and neutrals.

Other forms of public law are constitutional law, the law of municipal corporations, the law of taxation, and to a large extent the law relating to administrative officers.

An important branch of public law is criminal law. It is public law because in their essential character all crimes are offenses against the public, although on its other side criminal law deals with the responsibility of private individuals for their criminal acts. Acts are crimes when in some manner they interfere with the public welfare and thus constitute offenses against the public. The crime may or may not be an actionable wrong against some other person and thus give rise to private rights in that person, that is to say, some acts may be both crimes and private wrongs. And of the actionable wrongs against private individuals, only those of a gross character, such as those involving violent interference with the person, the taking of property without consent, fraud, etc., are deemed sufficiently injurious to the public as a whole to warrant treating them as criminal. It is obvious that generally speaking there can be no crime without the commission of an act of such a character that the courts deem it in itself sufficiently injurious to the state to warrant its criminal prosecution and punishment.

Criminal law, therefore, like other branches of the law, deals only with acts, and it pays no attention to the morals, intentions, or motives of mankind, unless they find expression in acts which the law deems injurious to the state and therefore criminal. On the other hand, the law may pay attention to incomplete acts if they are of a criminal nature and come dangerously near completion. It is upon this theory that attempts to commit crime which for one reason or another fail of their purpose are nevertheless themselves treated as criminal.

As, however, the end sought by a criminal prosecution is the punishment of the offender, the law makes inquiry into his moral accountability for his criminal act, and generally does not hold him guilty of crime and consequently punishable unless such accountability exists in the form of so-called "criminal intent." Thus, the state may be injured by the accidental killing of one of its citizens, or by an accidental injury to or the destruction of property, quite as much as when those injuries are the result of design, but the law does not deem those acts crimes unless they are accompanied by such mental state as would render the doer of them morally responsible for his acts.

Just what constitutes intent cannot be comprehensively stated in a brief discussion. At the outset, however, it should be noted that criminal intent should not be confounded with motive. The nature of the motive with which a criminal act is done is generally immaterial. It will be no defense to the charge of polygamy that the person was actuated by a deeply religious motive; or to one charged with disturbing the public peace that he was engaged in conducting a religious meeting. Nor, on the other hand, does bad motive render criminal an act otherwise innocent. Motives, of course, may be material as some proof that a defendant committed the act with which he is charged, where it is shown that the defendant was under a strong motive to commit that act. In such a case, however, motive is not directly involved; it is only incidental to proving the commission of the act with which the defendant is charged. Nor does criminal law presuppose any knowledge on the part of the defendant of the law rendering any given act criminal. Indeed, there are cases on record of conviction for a crime under a newly enacted statute, the existence of which could not possibly have been known to the defendant at the time of his act.

It is said sometimes, that one is presumed to know the law, which is a misstatement of the principle, adopted on grounds of policy, that ignorance of the law is no excuse or defense to one charged with crime. In its last analysis, therefore, criminal intent in the case of a defendant of sane mind is nothing more than knowledge on his part that he is doing an act which the law deems criminal, coupled with the will to do it. Any facts or circumstances which prevent the existence of such knowledge prevent the existence of criminal intent. Thus, the taking of another's property under the mistaken belief that it is the taker's own, the killing of a friend under the mistaken belief that one is necessarily repelling a burglar, are examples of want of criminal intent because of want of the requisite knowledge.

This definition of intent, however, is subject to two limitations: first, the rule based upon sound public policy that one who intends to do an act criminal in its nature and who voluntarily engages in the doing of it is liable for all its consequences, even though they be such as could not have been foreseen. Thus, one who commits an assault resulting in the death of the person assaulted is criminally liable for homicide, even though the assault was one which could not have been reasonably expected to cause death. The second modification is to be found in a certain class of crimes in which there is associated with the act some special state of mind which must exist in addition to mere knowledge of the act which the law defines as criminal. Thus, in order to constitute the crime of larceny, the offender must not only take another's property and know that he is taking it, but the taking must be with the intent or purpose to appropriate the property to the taker's own use. If the intent or purpose to appropriate another's property is not present in the mind of the defendant, the crime is not committed, although he did the act essential to the commission of the crime and knew that he was doing it. It follows that when specific intent is a necessary part of a crime, any mistake, whether it be a mistake of law or fact which prevents the existence of that intent, will prevent the crime from coming into existence.

Thus, if A under a mistake of law believes that B's goods are A's own, and acting on that belief takes them, he is not guilty of larceny, because the intent to appropriate another's goods to his own use did not exist, and an essential element of the crime was therefore wanting.

This intent, which in this class of crimes must coexist with the act and knowledge of it, is sometimes spoken of as specific intent, and crimes in which specific intent is an essential element are spoken of as crimes of specific intent. The great number of statutory crimes which forbid the wilful or malicious doing of an act are types of crimes of specific intent. Murder in the first degree is under certain circumstances also a crime of specific intent, because the person charged with murder in the first degree must not only be shown to have committed the act of killing another, but he must have done the act with the intent or design to cause death. Whenever, however, one assaults another and causes his death without intending to produce that result he may be guilty of manslaughter only, which is a crime of general intent, since the only elements of the crime are the act constituting the assault, the knowledge and will to commit it, and the consequent death of the victim.

It is, of course, quite competent for legislatures to dispense with intent in crimes, and it is not unusual for statutes defining mere police regulations to dispense, either expressly or by judicial construction, with criminal intent as an element in crime. Thus statutes imposing penalties for unlawful possession of game in the closed season, for selling or having in possession adulterated food or false weights or measures, are interpreted in many states as dispensing with criminal intent, and one may be convicted of violating the statute, although he is quite innocent of any intention of doing the prohibited act.

Our criminal law, like most other branches of the law, has been inherited from the English law on the subject; but it has generally undergone great statutory modifications in most of the United States.

There are three general types of legislation. One, as in Massachusetts, merely supplements the common law of crimes, which continues in full force, except as limited or repealed in a minor degree by statute. Another, as in New York, provides that only the offenses designated by statute are criminal, but permits reference to the common law, in order properly to define and interpret the language of the statute. In still a third class, as in Louisiana, the acts constituting crimes are required both to be designated and defined by statute.

Early in its history the Supreme Court of the United States decided that the Federal courts had no common law criminal jurisdiction. That Congress, however, has authority to make criminal by statutes acts injurious to the Federal government has never been doubted, so that all offenses against the Federal government must be designated as criminal by Federal statutes, before the courts will take cognizance of them, although under the decisions of the Federal courts reference may be made to the common law in interpreting the Federal statutory law of crimes.

The ultimate aim of criminal prosecution is, of course, the punishment of the offender. In its origin it is believed that the purpose of punishment was primarily vengeance. Indeed, our criminal law had its origin in the judicial recognition of the private right of vengeance which seems to have characterized primitive systems of law. At a later period the idea of the prevention of crime entered into the theory of punishment, and to-day special emphasis is laid on the reform of the criminal, in meting out punishment to him.

All of these elements are important in determining the kind of punishment and the method of carrying it out, for although we all recognize the necessity of prevention of crime and if possible the reform of the criminal, a punishment which does not adequately take into account the public sense of wrong and injury will prove to be the germ of loss of respect for law, and the beginning of public disorder.

It remains for us now to consider the important branch of English law known as equity. In a general sense equity means fairness, and is sometimes used to denote the exercise of discretion, which within certain limits may be allowed to a judge in the application of rules of law so as to prevent their harsh operation. By equity, used in its technical sense, however, we mean the peculiar system of law developed by the English Court of Chancery, which has been completely incorporated into our jurisprudence in the United States. We shall best understand its nature and origin by directing attention to certain peculiarities of the common law which brought about — or at least greatly encouraged — the development of equity.

The common law from early times was administered by the King's Courts presided over by judges appointed by the Crown, and aided in later times by a jury. As we have already seen, in an action brought at common law, when the remedy sought is the payment of money as damages or compensation for the invasion of the plaintiff's right by the defendant, the result of the action must always be a judgment for the payment of money, either that the plaintiff recover, or, if he fail, that the costs of the litigation be paid by plaintiff to the defendant. In either case, if payment be not made, the mandate of the court is issued to the sheriff, directing him to satisfy the judgment by a levy upon and sale of the property of the unsuccessful party.

Since a judgment at law affects only the property of the parties to the litigation, it is sometimes spoken of as a judgment *in rem.* The weakness, as well as the strength of such a system of procedure is apparent. To avail one's self of a legal remedy, one must wait until his rights have been interfered with and he has suffered some legal damage. The courts of law had no machinery by which a threatened wrong could be prevented or by which a defendant could be compelled to do the specific thing he was legally obligated to do.

If the unsuccessful litigant had no property, or concealed it, or removed it from the jurisdiction of the court, the court of law was powerless to enforce its judgments. Moreover, the form of the judgment at law necessarily limited the litigation to two-sided controversies. Although there might be three or more persons involved in the litigation, all must be arrayed on one side or the other as plaintiff or defendant. There was no possibility of a many-sided controversy, as where land is partitioned among several heirs, or a mortgage is foreclosed and there are numerous parties interested in the mortgaged property. This inherent weakness in the system of law administered by the King's Court necessarily resulted in petitions to the crown for relief in those cases where, because of these defects, the King's Courts were unable to afford an adequate remedy. In cases where the law could give no relief, or where for some of the reasons stated the relief at law was inadequate, these petitions were presented on the theory that the king, who, according to medieval theory, was the source of all justice, could do justice, even when his courts failed because of the peculiarities of their organization.

Petitions of this character were normally referred to the chancellor, who was keeper of the Great Seal and vested with royal authority, and who was usually a powerful ecclesiastic. If the case was one for which there was no adequate legal remedy, the chancellor could, on conscientious grounds, as it was said, command in the king's name the defendant to do or not to do something, as justice might require, and thus give a remedy when there was none at law. Originally, of course, such petitions were irregular in form and substance, and while the relief afforded could not be said to be capricious, it was in no sense systematic. Gradually, however, a practice which was irregular and sporadic in the beginning became little by little the common method of invoking the aid of the crown when the petitioner was without adequate legal remedy. Ultimately all such petitions for extraordinary relief were addressed directly to the chancellor in accordance with definite forms and rules of procedure, and the relief granted was in accordance with definite juristic principles, so that by the time of the reign of Queen Elizabeth, the chancellor's court was as firmly established as a court administering justice according to the principles of equity, as were the King's Courts during that and previous reigns. As the system developed, the decrees of the chancellor or of the vice-chancellors, who were appointed to assist him, came to have the force of precedents, just as in the case of judicial decisions of the King's Courts, although in Chancery, as the chancellor's or equity court was called, a wider latitude was given to judicial discretion than was exercised by the law courts.

The distinguishing feature of equity is that the chancellor, or equity judge, who, because of his official position, originally had delegated to him the royal prerogative of command, has power to command things to be done or not to be done. That is, the equity courts act *in personam*, as it is said, or against the person, as distinguished from the law courts whose jurisdiction is *in rem* or over the property by the litigants. Thus, the chancellor could enjoin the defendant from committing a threatened injury to the plaintiff's property, or make a decree directing the defendant to convey property to the plaintiff in accordance with his contract. If the defendant failed to obey, he could be punished for contempt by imprisonment until he became obedient to the court. As a consequence of this method of exercising authority the chancellor could prevent threatened wrongs by injunction. He could dispose of many-sided controversies, since he could command each of the parties to do whatever the justice of the case might require. If jurisdiction was once acquired over the person of the defendant, he could be commanded to convey or otherwise dispose of property, regardless of its location, although in all of these cases courts of law would be powerless to render any effective judgment.

Another characteristic of equity due to its origin was that its jurisdiction was exercised only when there was no legal remedy, or when the legal remedy was inadequate. Equity thus set up its own standard of justice and ultimately came to recognize that rights recognized as valid and enforceable at law might be exercised in an unconscientious and inequitable manner, and therefore that such exercise of them might be prohibited by equity. Law, as we have seen in previous chapters, laid its emphasis upon right. Equity directed its attention to inquiring whether a right acquired or conferred upon an individual by law had been unconscientiously acquired or was being unconscientiously exercised by that individual. The emphasis in equity, therefore, was laid on the morality or conscientiousness of conduct, and hence on obligations growing out of such conduct. It therefore reserved the right to prevent or restrain the exercise of a legal right whenever in the judgment of the courts of equity such exercise was unconscientious.

Thus, law and equity at many points came into apparent conflict. This conflict, however, was more apparent than real, since courts of equity never interfered directly with the courts of law by the process of injunction; that is, the chancellor did not assume to tell the judge of a court of law what he should or should not do, but the chancellor would, in a proper case, prohibit the owner of legal rights from enforcing them in a court of law, if to do so would be an unconscientious use of the owner's legal rights. It was thus that courts of equity developed the law of trusts, the fundamental conception of which is that one vested with all the legal rights in property may nevertheless be bound in equity to hold and administer property for the benefit of another. Thus we see that equity not only exercised its jurisdiction to protect legal rights, but that it created new classes of rights, wholly equitable in character, that is to say, recognized and enforced only in courts of equity and measured by what the chancellors deemed conscientious conduct on the part of the defendants summoned before them.

The way in which equity expanded its jurisdiction by the creation of new equitable rights, and thus softened the rigors of the common law system, may be illustrated by some account of the history of the jurisdiction of equity over mortgages. At common law a mortgage was a conveyance of land by the mortgagor to the mortgagee, with a conditional right in the mortgagor to reënter and repossess himself of the land upon payment of the mortgage debt. Since the right of reëntry was upon condition of payment of the mortgage indebtedness at a specified time, it could be exercised according to the legal rules only on strict performance of the condition. If, therefore, the mortgagor defaulted in payment of interest, or was even a day late in the payment of principal of the mortgage debt, his right of reëntry was lost and the mortgagee became the undisputed owner of the property. Equity, however, readily found a way to avoid such a harsh result. Since the conveyance was made as security only for the payment of the debt, no injustice would be done to the mortgagee if he were compelled to give up the mortgaged property upon payment of the mortgage debt, principal and interest. The mortgagor in default was therefore permitted by equity to file his bill or petition to redeem the mortgaged property on payment of the mortgage debt in full by compelling the mortgagee, who was legally entitled to the mortgaged property, to reconvey it to the mortgagor. The first examples of the exercise of this kind of jurisdiction by courts of equity are found in the early years of the reign of Charles I, about 1622. It would be difficult to find a more revolutionary development in the history of the law than the application in this way of the principle of the courts of equity that it would not permit one to make an unconscientious and unjust use of a legal right merely for the benefit or enrichment of the person so exercising it.

Since, however, it was neither convenient nor just that mortgagees should be perpetually subject to bills to redeem, and as a method of finally settling the rights of the parties, the chancellor established the equitable right in the mortgagee to file a bill praying that the mortgage be foreclosed by cutting off the right of the mortgagor to redeem unless within a certain time fixed by the chancellor the mortgage indebtedness was paid in full. The first examples of a bill to foreclose are found in the reign of Charles I, about 1625.

Later on mortgages were foreclosed, as is now the practice, by a judicial sale of the mortgaged property, the proceeds being used to pay the mortgage debt and the expenses of sale, any amount remaining as surplus being turned over to the mortgagor. Equity in this manner developed an independent system of extraordinary remedies applicable not only to mortgagor and mortgagee, but to many other relationships which not only afforded protection to suitors when legal remedies were inadequate, but prevented the inequitable or unconscientious exercise of legal rights and thus created new equitable remedies unknown to the common law system.

The English equity system was transferred to most of our colonies and now exists in those states which have adopted the common law system. In New Jersey the equity system, administered by a chancellor and vice-chancellors, exists as a system separate from the common law system, which is administered by separate courts substantially as the two systems were administered in England down to the enactment of the Judicature Act in 1875. By this Act the courts of chancery and the common law courts were consolidated and the same judges were given authority to sit both at law and in equity. In our Federal courts the two systems are administered separately in separate courts, which, however, are presided over by the same judges. Very generally, however, in the United States, the two systems are administered together by the same courts, presided over by the same judges and by means of a uniform procedure. In New York, by the Constitution of 1846 the separate court of Chancery was abolished and our Supreme Court was established with jurisdiction in law and in equity.

This so-called merger of law and equity is frequently spoken of as though it had abolished the distinction between the two forms of remedy. It has, of course, materially affected the procedure in equity cases, but no legislative fiat could destroy the essential difference between the nature of rights developed by courts of law and of those of equitable origin. Nor could it eradicate the fundamental differences in the remedies afforded by the two systems. It is therefore still necessary for the student of law to master the principles of equity and to know something of its origin and history in order to prepare himself for the practice of his profession, and to contribute to the growth and development of law through the expansion of equitable remedies.

As we have seen, one of the remedies afforded by equity courts was the prevention of threatened wrongs by injunction restraining a threatened tort, or by preserving the *status quo* pending the final determination of the rights of the parties. This is accomplished by the preliminary injunction, or the injunction *pendente lite*. This injunction is granted by the court before a hearing is had on the merits of the controversy between the parties, in order to protect the plaintiff from irreparable injury while his case is in process of being heard and disposed of by the court. If a defendant threatens to cut down the plaintiff's shade trees or to tear down his house or to destroy his business, legal relief by way of damages would be of little avail if the court permitted the defendant to go on doing the wrongful acts until the final hearing and decree.

Under modern practice the preliminary injunction is granted on affidavits submitted by the plaintiff which must show that the defendant is threatening to do unlawful acts injurious to the plaintiff, and that if they are not restrained pending the litigation, the plaintiff will suffer irreparable injury. Security may be and usually is required of the plaintiff to compensate the defendant for loss or damage resulting to him, if ultimately the plaintiff's right to an injunction is not upheld. If an injunction is granted without hearing the defendant, the procedure is such that the defendant may thereafter be heard and affidavits may be submitted in his behalf for the purpose of modifying or vacating the injunction. Or the court may, if it choose, take testimony of witnesses with respect to the facts of the case before deciding what relief shall be granted.

Thus applied the remedy by injunction is one of the most salutary afforded by the law and is essential to the orderly administration of justice if it is to protect the weak and law-abiding from lawless aggression.

A few years ago there was a decided tendency toward limiting the power of courts to issue preliminary injunctions and to punish for contempt, particularly in the case of labor disputes and in actions brought to restrain governmental officers from carrying into effect legislation or orders of public service commissions reducing the rates of public service companies. In 1913 Congress passed an act providing that in the latter class of cases an injunction should only be granted after hearing before three Federal judges. Similar legislation restricting the power to issue injunctions in labor disputes introduced into Congress in 1913 failed of enactment.

By the so-called Clayton Act, enacted by Congress October 15, 1914, it was provided that no restraining order or injunction issued in labor disputes should prohibit any person or persons from ceasing to work or from persuading others by peaceful means to do so or from doing any other lawful acts; it was also provided that trial for contempt of injunction orders issued in labor disputes should be by jury, if the defendant so requires.

Legislation purporting to restrict the power of courts to issue injunctions in labor disputes has been enacted in some of the western states. In most cases, however, this legislation seems not to have substantially changed the law as it already existed in most of the United States and the indications are that the fear of government by injunction has markedly subsided within the past two years.

During the years 1902 to 1912, inclusive, twenty-six injunctions in labor disputes were granted by the Federal courts, while 704 injunctions were granted by those courts in other classes of cases. In substantially all, the acts enjoined were clearly illegal in character, and if not restrained, would have resulted in irreparable injury to the plaintiffs. To have withheld from such acts the restraining hand of the court would have resulted in a substantial denial of justice to the plaintiffs in those cases. As was said by Mr. Justice Brewer, in an address delivered in Brooklyn in 1909: —

> "Government by injunction has been an object of easy denunciation. So far from restricting its power, there never was a time when its unrestricted and vigorous exercise was worth more to the nation and for the best interests of all. As population becomes more dense, as business interests multiply and crowd each other, the restraining power of a court of equity is of far greater importance than a punishing power of criminal law. The best scientific thought of the day is along the lines of prevention rather than those of cure. We aim to stay the spread of epidemics rather than to permit them to run their course and attend solely to the work of curing the sick. And shall it be said of the law, which claims to be the perfection of reason and to express the highest thought of the day, that it no longer aims to prevent the wrong, but limits its action to the matter of punishment?
>
> "To take away the equitable power of restraining wrong is a step backward toward barbarism rather than a step forward toward a higher civilization. . . . Courts make mistakes in granting injunctions. So they do in other orders, and decrees. Shall the judicial power be taken away because of their occasional mistakes? The argument would lead to the total abolition of the judicial function."

Provision of statute or by rule of court which authorizes the courts to grant the injunction only on notice or if without notice only on the presentation of affidavits showing that irreparable injury would probably result to the plaintiff if such notice of his application were given to the defendant would seem, however, to be a reasonable restriction on the power of injunction and would tend to prevent judicial error.

Failure to obey the injunction subjects the offender to punishment for contempt by fine or imprisonment or both. By the ancient equitable procedure jurisdiction to try and punish for contempt rested exclusively with the judge. This power is still exercised by the judge except where modified or limited by statute as already indicated.

It would be difficult to overstate the importance of equity as supplementing the remedies afforded by the common law courts and as a medium for expanding and developing our legal system. The remedy by injunction, the creation of the system of trusts, the recognition of the principle that the untrammeled exercise of legal rights may be subjected to equitable limitations, are typical of the methods by which the chancellors gave to our legal system elasticity and brought the rules of law more closely into harmony with the principles of morality. The growth of the equity system through the gradual conversion of a purely administrative office into a court exercising judicial powers was, of course, anomalous, and due to historical causes. The fact, however, that equity principles were developed in a separate court, whose freedom of action was unembarrassed by legal rules, undoubtedly facilitated the expansion of equity and thus made it a more effective agency in grafting on to our legal system the notion that even legal rights might be subjected to equitable limitations based on moral principles. In most states the equity system has now become completely incorporated into the legal system, so that to-day our law is the resultant of this amalgamation whereby the principles of the common law have been combined with and to some extent modified by the principles of equity.

V

PROCEDURE

One may have a right which his lawyer advises him that the law will recognize and protect, yet it is necessary, before he can invoke the aid of the law, to set its machinery in motion in order to secure its protection. Courts do not act of their own motion or take any action apart from the controversies which are regularly brought before them for determination.

If A conceives that he has a right against B which B denies, A if he would assert his right must apply to the court having authority to determine the cause, for its protection and relief. When the matter is brought before the court some form of trial must take place in order that the respective claims of the parties may be heard and passed upon. If the judgment is for A, the plaintiff, it must be enforced against the defendant in one of a variety of ways, depending on the nature of the judgment. If it is the usual judgment for the recovery of money, the court issues its mandate to the sheriff, directing him to seize the defendant's property, sell it in the manner provided by law, and apply the proceeds in the satisfaction of the judgment.

This process, by which a party brings his case into court, conducts its trial, and secures and enforces the judgment of the court, is known as procedure. All the law of procedure therefore relates to the process of securing one's rights in court and is thus merely incidental to the law defining one's rights which is known as substantive law. The necessity and importance of the law of procedure will at once become apparent when one considers the many procedural steps which must be taken in enforcing one's rights in court.

Before the plaintiff can present his case to the court the defendant must be brought legally before the court and given an opportunity to defend. This is accomplished by the issuance by the court of its process called a writ of right or summons, commanding him to appear and answer the plaintiff's complaint, and when this is served upon the defendant, the court is authorized to proceed with the adjudication of the cause. It may be that the plaintiff requires some preliminary relief before final judgment, for example, an attachment of the defendant's goods, so that the sheriff may take and hold them for the purpose of satisfying from them any judgment which the plaintiff may finally obtain or an injunction commanding the defendant not to interfere with the plaintiff's rights, pending the trial or the appointment of a receiver whose duty it is to take into possession and preserve property which is the subject of controversy. In either case the plaintiff must apply to the court for its order upon sufficient proof by affidavit to entitle him to the relief sought and at some stage of the proceedings the defendant must be given opportunity to be heard upon the question of the plaintiff's right to the preliminary relief which he seeks. Before the trial the plaintiff must state in a document, called a pleading, the facts upon which he relies as entitling him to legal relief. To this the defendant must interpose a written answer stating his defense. In a variety of ways the defendant may deny the facts upon which the plaintiff relies, or he may deny that the facts upon which the plaintiff relies give rise to any legal right in the plaintiff against the defendant. When the facts are in dispute a trial results, in the course of which a jury is selected to act as judges of fact. Testimony of witnesses is taken by means of question and answer, which must conform to legal rules of evidence. The case is then submitted to the jury with instructions as to the law of the case by the judge. The jury returns its verdict, upon the basis of which the final judgment of the court is entered. At various stages of the litigation proceedings may be had for the correction of error, for compelling either party to conform his procedure to the rules of law, and for appeals to a higher court. Appeals may be taken from the final judgment, and in many cases two and in rarer instances three appeals may be had. This, in briefest outline, is the course of the usual litigation of importance. There may be many variations of what I have termed the usual course, and if the appeal results in the direction of a new trial, the whole procedure may be gone through with a second time; and there are not a few cases on record where new trials have been directed three and even four or more times.

In criminal trials the procedure is somewhat simpler. The state or the commonwealth must state its complaint against the defendant in an indictment found by the grand jury consisting of not more than 23 nor less than 16 grand jurymen sitting in the county where the alleged offense was committed. The defendant, when arraigned, must plead to the indictment, the plea being oral, and "not guilty" if he wishes to defend. No appeal lies from a verdict for the defendant, because of the rule that a person may not be twice placed in jeopardy for the same offense. There are, however, liberal provisions for appeal by the defendant, in case the verdict goes against him, and for testing the legality of his conviction, and the fairness of his trial.

I apprehend from what I have said about procedure that you will be inclined to think that the client's rights are made to depend too much on mere questions of procedure, and that the lawyer's time, as well as the client's, is too much occupied in applying rules of procedure rather than the rules which relate to the substance of his cause. That has been the layman's criticism of legal procedure at most periods in the history of the law and I regret to say that there have been few periods in its history when there was not much justification for the criticism. I believe that this fact is explained partly by difficulties inherent in organizing a system of procedure which will succeed in adequately protecting the rights of litigants without becoming highly technical, not to say burdensome, partly because of historical influences affecting our system of procedure and partly because the effort toward accomplishing reform has been largely misdirected.

Historically, the form of procedure has had a tremendous influence upon the common law both substantive and procedural. The very existence of substantive rights — that is, legal rights in the sense in which we have previously referred to them — in any given case very often depends upon whether the facts of the case are such as would formerly have conformed to the essential allegation of some recognized form of action as it was established in the early history of the common law. So that much light is thrown on the present state of the common law by a study of the early forms of pleading and procedure.

For example, the present law that all contracts must be founded upon consideration which is a detriment or surrender of a right given in exchange for the defendant's promise, is directly traceable to the technical requirements of pleadings in the early history of the law. The right to recover money paid to a defendant by mistake or to recover money or the value of property acquired by the defendant by tort or fraud, had its origin in a rule of pleading, that a plaintiff might state in his declaration or complaint a fictitious promise on the part of the defendant and prove the allegation in his pleading by showing any facts establishing a legal liability to pay the money claimed regardless of any actual promise by the defendant. The plaintiff was deemed to have proved the defendant's promise by proving his legal liability, although he did not show that the defendant had ever actually made a promise, either expressly or impliedly, to pay money to the plaintiff. Once the pleader recognized the utility of this fiction, the possibility of expanding remedies in quasi-contracts (that is, rights to recover liquidated sums of money when the defendant had entered into no contract) was practically unlimited.

Many of the peculiarities of the law relating to right to recover the possession of real estate, or money for its use and occupation, are directly traceable to peculiarities of procedure by which rights relating to real estate are enforced. These examples, which are typical of many others which might be given, suffice to illustrate the constant and prevailing influence of the law of pleading of the past on our present view of substantive law.

Common law procedure was developed during a period when in all human activities great emphasis was laid on formalism. The form of a transaction was thus often quite as important and significant as its substance. This tendency found its expression in all early systems of law in various formal acts, the legal validity and effectiveness of which depended on their form, regardless of their substance. Thus, the transfer of title to real estate has always been attended by certain formalities, in order to make the transfer effectual, no matter how certain the intention of the grantor. Unless the proper ceremony for transfer of the real estate was performed, his intention would not become effectual. Covenants, in order to be binding, must be solemnized by a seal affixed by the covenantor, in order to make his promise legally binding. The creation of various estates in lands must be accompanied by the use of certain formal language in order to create the estate intended. In many cases legal ceremony was justifiable because of the added solemnity given by it to transactions of importance. But often the only explanation of the emphasis laid upon form was the mental habit of the men of learning during the early history of the law, and particularly during the fifteenth, sixteenth, and seventeenth centuries.

This tendency toward legal formalism reached its height in the system of procedure at common law. The authority to hear and determine a controversy at common law was vested in the King's Courts in each case by the issuance of a writ of summons or original writ, as it was called, from the office of the chancellor, who, as the personal representative of the king, had authority to command the defendant to appear in court and answer the plaintiff's complaint. The writ was thus both the royal authority for the court to try the case and a command to the defendant to render unto the plaintiff his due, or else to appear and defend against his claim.

From very early times there were in use in chancery a number of forms of writs supposed to correspond exactly to all of the various forms of recognized legal rights. There was thus a writ of trespass for trespass upon realty, a writ of trespass to personalty, a writ of trespass to the person, various forms of writ for the possession of realty, a writ of detinue for the wrongful detention of personal property, the writ of debt for the recovery of a common law debt, at a later date the writ of assumpsit for breach of simple contract, and the writ of case, or of action on the case, as it was called, where the plaintiff sought to recover for injuries in tort, as for negligence, libel, slander, etc. In all there were some forty recognized forms of common law writs, in common use, each highly technical in character, having a distinct form of its own, and these were supposed collectively to cover the whole field of legal rights.

When the plaintiff had once chosen his form of writ, his declaration, that is, the pleading in which he stated his cause of action, must conform to the writ, so that for every form of writ there was a corresponding form of declaration. The plaintiff must needs state his cause of action in one of the established forms of pleading. One might have a perfectly good cause of action, yet if he mistook his writ and the corresponding form of pleading, there was no opportunity for correcting his mistake, but judgment must go against him. He might or might not begin over again, according to the nature of his mistake, but in any event, there was loss of time and effort and money, and in many cases a substantial denial of justice.

Assuming that the plaintiff chose the proper form of action, the whole system of pleading was devised so as to bring the parties to a single issue of law or fact. That is, the defendant might deny some or all of the facts in the plaintiff's declaration, or he might admit them and set up new facts which he conceived destroyed the legal effect of the plaintiff's alleged cause of action, to which in turn the plaintiff might interpose a second pleading, either by way of denial, or setting up new matter. Thus, in an action of debt upon a bond, the defendant might plead a release, to which the plaintiff might interpose a pleading known as a replication, setting up that the release was procured by duress or fraud, to which the defendant might plead again by way of rejoinder denying the duress or fraud. It was the aim of the common law system of pleading to carry the successive pleadings to a stage where the facts alleged on one side were denied on the other. The parties were then said to be at issue and the disputed issue of fact was in due course tried before a jury. The pleadings beginning with that of the plaintiff were known as the declaration, plea, replication, rebutter, surrebutter, rejoinder, and surrejoinder. Beyond the surrejoinder the pleadings had no distinctive names and were seldom employed.

Either party might at any stage of the pleading interpose a demurrer, as it was called, the effect of which was to admit the facts alleged in the preceding pleading, but to deny their sufficiency in law as a cause of action or defense for the pleader. The effect of the demurrer, therefore, was to raise an issue of law for decision by the court. Thus, if the plaintiff demurred to the defendant's plea, the question for the court was whether the defendant's plea was legally a good defense to the cause of action stated in the declaration. If the demurrer was sustained, then judgment must go for the plaintiff. If overruled, the judgment must go for the defendant. The whole procedure of pleading was devoted to bringing the parties to a single issue of fact or law, and to this end all the resources and technicality of the legal art were devoted. It might happen through the error of the pleader that the issue actually raised by the pleadings was immaterial or not the real issue between the parties. Nevertheless, the controversy must be determined in accordance with the determination of the single issue raised by the pleadings. Thus it was not unusual, because of the error of the pleader, for a cause to be determined not in accordance with its real merits, but upon the basis of an immaterial or collateral matter, and the case, as it was said, "went off" on a point of pleading. The whole system abounded with refinements, subtleties, and technicalities, which made the preparation of pleadings and practice papers one of the most difficult of arts.

Criminal pleading, that is, the form of indictment at common law, was also highly technical, but for somewhat different reasons. The pleadings in criminal law were less involved than in civil cases, since there was only a single plea to the indictment and this did not aim at singleness of issue. The indictment, however, was more formal, if possible, than the civil pleading. Particular crimes must be described in a particular way and with the use of certain prescribed words; thus, an indictment for felony was required to contain the words "feloniously" or the defendant would go free. The indictment must conclude with the words "against the peace of the king." The indictment for arson must contain the word "burn." The indictment for murder must contain the word "murder." Omission of these words was fatal to the indictment, however accurately the pleader may have described the crimes charged. At the trial the prosecution was required to prove the commission of the offense in the exact manner alleged in the indictment, failing which, the conviction could not be sustained.

These and many other technical rules of procedure were due not only to the passion for formalism during the formative period of the system, but to what we would now consider an exaggerated tenderness for defendants charged with crime. The oppressive use of the machinery of criminal law in early English history, and the excessive punishment meted out to criminals, led courts to build many technical safeguards around the person of the man charged with crime. There was thus a historical reason and justification for the technicality in criminal procedure which did not exist in the case of civil procedure, and which has tended to make the technicalities of criminal procedure outlive those on the civil side of the court.

The fact that under the common law system of procedure, both civil and criminal, there could and did frequently occur substantial failures of justice which were irremediable, led to belated reforms in the early part of the last century by the adoption of the so-called Hilary Rules of Practice, in 1834. These rules, applicable only to civil procedure, were adopted by the judges of the English courts at the so-called Hilary Term of Court, from which they received their name, and they were the first of a long series of remedial measures taken for the purpose of making the system of pleading and procedure less technical, less difficult of application, and less likely to result in injustice to suitors. This and most later reforms have sought to accomplish two great ends: one was the prevention of failures of justice by allowing greater freedom of amendment; the other was the simplification of the system of procedure so that it might be more easily applied with less expenditure of time and effort and with less requirement of highly specialized technical training on the part of the lawyer. I think it may be fairly said that the first end has been generally achieved. There is no jurisdiction, so far as I am aware, where there is substantial ultimate failure of justice in civil cases because of the system of procedure employed.

In criminal procedure there is, of course, no possibility of correction of any substantial error by amendment of the indictment. In most states the grand jury alone has power to find an indictment under our system. If, therefore, an indictment does not properly charge a crime in substance, the court and district attorney are powerless to correct the error. The only course is for the grand jury to re-indict. The reform of criminal procedure, therefore, has necessarily been limited to simplifying the form of the indictment and dispensing with its technical requirements, so long as it states the substance of the crime charged. This is the effect of the reformed statutory procedure adopted in New York. Under the English criminal law system there was no appeal from a conviction until within the last few years, when Parliament adopted the Criminal Appeal Act. In this country, however, appeals have always been allowed with great liberality.

Both courts and legislatures in the United States have been more tardy in sweeping away the wilderness of technicalities behind which a defendant charged with a crime may take refuge, and in recent years we have had in some of the middle western states some glaring examples of failures of criminal justice because of the adherence to technical, outworn rules of criminal pleading and procedure. I do not think, however, that this criticism is one which can now be made generally. There are at the present time few states where persons charged with crimes escape conviction because of technicalities of procedure. To satisfy my interest on this point I have examined the reports of homicide cases in the past ten years in several typical states. The states selected were New York, New Jersey, Pennsylvania, Massachusetts, Illinois, and California. The record is as follows:

	Number of Affirmations	Number of Reversals
New York	71	16
New Jersey	14	2
Massachusetts	14	none
Pennsylvania	71	16
Illinois	75	31
California	40	12

Practically without exception the reversals were not directed on technical grounds, but because there had been actual unfairness in the trial which was prejudicial to the interests of the defendant. That so large a number of reversals should have been necessary in those states having an elected judiciary is undoubtedly a reflection upon the efficiency of the trial courts; but the fault in these jurisdictions, at least, seems not to have been properly chargeable to the technical character of criminal procedure.

These and other data readily available to those who prefer accurate information to guesswork or mere impression demonstrate that the failures of justice in criminal cases because of technicalities of procedure are much less frequent than is commonly supposed. There are several organizations at the present time engaged in the work of preparing a reformed system of criminal procedure, whose aim is mainly to abolish technical requirements in the indictment and to avoid the necessity of reindictment, or discharge of the prisoner when the state fails to prove completely and minutely the offense in the precise manner and form alleged in the indictment. At a conference of lawyers interested in the administration of criminal law which I attended lately in New York City, I was gratified to learn how little occasion there was for the adoption of this reform both in this state and a very considerable number of others. I believe that this system, or one substantially like it, will be adopted in those states having need of reform in criminal procedure at no distant date.

There are, of course, reforms in the administration of criminal law which in the judgment of competent critics require the careful study and attention of those who desire to improve the methods of fixing responsibility for crime. Such, for example, as allowing the jury to consider the failure of a defendant to testify in his own behalf, requiring a defendant charged with crime to answer questions of the district attorney or public prosecutor, authorizing a conviction of crime by less than the unanimous verdict of a petit jury. These are, however, matters of substance, rather than of mere formal procedure, and will be referred to in the chapter on law reform.

In the effort to secure simplification of civil procedure, we have not been as fortunate. The experience in New York may be taken as typical of that of a good many other jurisdictions. In 1848 the effort to simplify procedure in this state bore fruit in the adoption by legislative enactment of a code of procedure prepared by David Dudley Field and commonly known as the Field Code. In 1876 this was revised and the revision enacted into the present Code of Civil Procedure. This code now consists of some 3500 sections of statute law, comprising over one thousand finely printed pages, all relating to procedure in the Supreme, City, County and Surrogate courts. To this code there have been added the 366 sections of the Municipal Court Code relating to procedure in the Municipal courts, 963 sections of the Code of Criminal Procedure regulating procedure in the criminal courts, and the 84 general rules of court which supplement the various provisions of the code. Thus, the efforts to simplify procedure in New York have resulted in the creation of some 5000 sections of written law, filling about 2000 printed pages. These laws, be it remembered, relate not to the substantive rights of individuals, but only to the process by which the individual may secure or protect his rights. The result of our efforts to render our legal procedure simple would be laughable were it not so tragic in its effect on the administration of justice.

But the trouble does not end with the mere mass of practice statutes which have been accumulated by successive legislative enactments since the adoption of the simplified procedure in 1848. At every session of the legislature hundreds of bills are introduced to amend the sections of the code or to add new sections. These bills are often crudely drawn without reference to the harmonious operation of new sections with old sections of the code or with the judicial interpretation of the amended sections. Many of these bills pass so that each year new sections are added to the code and the old sections undergo revision which is rarely scientific and is usually crude and haphazard.

Thus, our Code of Civil Procedure, ponderous and complex as it was at the beginning, is constantly increasing in size and complexity. In the past twenty years 1600 sections of the code have been amended; some of them many times. The effort to regulate every procedural step explicitly and minutely has greatly increased the burden of practice, and has resulted in constant resort to the courts for judicial settlement of questions which might well have been left to the discretion and good sense of counsel and which could never have arisen under the highly technical common law system.

A well-known lawyer has made a compilation of practice statistics on the basis of which he concludes that under the existing procedure in New York, at least 60 per cent of the decisions of our courts relate exclusively to points of practice. This has been interpreted by him to mean that the chances of a meritorious case being disposed of on a point of practice rather than on its merits are as three to two. This, of course, is an erroneous conclusion, for the determination of a point of practice, one way or the other, does not necessarily mean that the final result of the case on the merits is affected adversely. It does mean, however, that an altogether disproportionate part of the time of the lawyer and the courts is devoted to the determination of questions which do not involve the substantial merits of the controversies which it is the purpose of courts to settle and that there is an enormous amount of lost motion and wasted effort in making progress toward the ultimate goal of justice for litigants.

How does it come about that the diligent and faithful effort to simplify our practice has had such a disastrous consequence?

Since 1848, when David Dudley Field drafted his code of three hundred and thirty-nine sections, there has been no lack of study and investigation of legal procedure. Our troubles are not due to neglect or to any underestimation of the importance of the subject; but because, I believe, we have disregarded the fundamental principles which must control the organization of any system of procedure if it is to be serviceable, without being so ponderous as to break down by its own weight.

The first consideration in the enactment of a code of procedure is a frank recognition of the fact that there is no royal method, either legislative or otherwise, whereby procedure may be rendered simple and effective in the hands of the practitioner too lazy or indifferent or incompetent to master the art of bringing his case into court and trying it in a simple, direct, and concise manner. The effort to prescribe by formal legislation minute regulations so that the practitioner may find in the code a rule for every contingency which may arise, is never ending. Once embarked on this course, new situations and the application of existing rules in a manner not foreseen demand perpetual legislative tinkering, until, as in our state to-day, the lawyer is lost in a wilderness of special, arbitrary, and rigid provisions, often inconsistent, or at least inharmonious, always changing and always increasing in number and complexity.

Again, any system of procedure, to be workable, must leave a great deal to judicial discretion, which is clearly impossible if the rules of practice are to be incorporated into rigid legislative provisions. Our code abounds in provisions prescribing in minutest detail the contents and form of affidavits, orders, notices, and other court papers. Failure to comply with these requirements frequently results in prolonged argument in court over mere matters of form or technical matters of practice leading, in many instances, to judicial determinations which would be unnecessary and unwarranted were it not for the express provisions of the code.

And, finally, the formulation of a system of procedure and its future amendment is primarily a matter for experts and preëminently for the judges themselves who are qualified by special training and experience for this important and delicate work. The perpetual tinkering of the code by the legislature, by amendments, which are usually crude in form, and seldom correlated with the other provisions of the code or with each other, would ultimately disorganize any system of procedure, however perfect in the beginning.

In each of these particulars the system of code procedure adopted in New York and a considerable number of states is radically at fault. It has sought to enact a final written rule to govern every case. In the simplest matters of procedure, little or nothing is left to the good sense and discretion of the court, and the whole scheme is subject to the vagaries of haphazard legislation which is often enacted without regard to the unity of the system as a whole or to the teachings of judicial experience.

The study of the New York code leaves one with a very distinct impression that in enacting it conscientious effort was made on the part of its framers to circumscribe the activities, in matters of practice, of the tricky and unscrupulous lawyer. The requirement that all proceedings, however insignificant, must be based on affidavits filed in court; that all proceedings must be taken in the exact manner prescribed and all notices given in a prescribed manner indicate that the authors of our code have very generally believed that they were preparing a system of procedure for a bar which could not be trusted to act honorably and conscientiously, according to the standards which prevail among gentlemen and which should indubitably characterize the members of a learned and honorable profession.

However commendable the desire to have a practice act which will protect the court and the bar from its unworthy members, the case is obviously one of attempting reform in the wrong place. To reform procedure by lowering its standards to the level of unworthy members of the bar reverses the process by which true reforms are to be attained. No system of procedure, however carefully prepared, will work well if those who apply it have low professional standards, and we might as well give up all efforts to secure a satisfactory system of procedure if we are not willing to begin with a thoroughgoing effort to reform the bar itself. Of this, I shall have more to say in a later lecture.

The view which has been expressed as to the elements which should characterize an adequate procedure points to the conclusion that the solution of the matter lies in the adoption of a constitutional provision by which the power and duty to formulate the rules governing procedure shall be delegated exclusively to the courts, which may be safely depended upon not to attempt to frame minute practice provisions to govern every case or deprive the court of sufficient discretion to decide matters on their merits, rather than in accordance with prescribed formal and technical rules. Above all, with such a provision in force, the perpetual amendment of our practice act by the inexpert would be at an end. The indications are not wanting that a reform of this kind is one of the results that may be hoped for by the approaching Constitutional Convention to be held in the state of New York.

The conditions which I have described as existing in New York exist in varying degree in many other states. In a few only have practice acts of substantially the character I have suggested been adopted. Notable among the latter is the state of Massachusetts, which has for many years had a short practice act, supplemented by rules of court. That this act has worked well is the universal opinion of lawyers who are familiar with it. Since the adoption of the Federal judiciary act of 1789 the practice of the Federal Equity Courts has been regulated almost exclusively by rules of court. Change of conditions has required their revision recently, but the ease, skill, and thoroughness with which the revision was accomplished, its brevity and adaptability to the needs of litigation, stand out in startling contrast to the results of our continuous amendment of the code by independent, sporadic legislative acts.

New Jersey has lately adopted a practice act authorizing supplementary rules of court. One of these rules provides:

"These rules shall be considered as general rules for the government of courts and the conduct of cases, and as the design of them is to facilitate business and to advance justice, they may be relaxed or dispensed with by the court in any case where it shall be manifest to the court that a strict adherence to them will work surprise or injustice."

This rule certainly states an ideal of procedure, toward which our efforts for reform should be directed. If it be suggested that such wide discretion gives opportunity for favoritism and judicial action proceeding from corrupt motives, then the obvious answer is that if our bench is unworthy to be entrusted with a procedure of this character, which emphatically I do not believe to be the case in New York, then we should elevate our bench to the best standards, and not lower our standards of procedure to the level of a degraded bench. Evidently in New Jersey, where the judges are appointed, there is no fear of giving to the judges those powers which must necessarily be incident to the competent administration of any system of justice.

The reform of a system of procedure is not a matter lightly to be undertaken. We have trained a generation of judges and lawyers under our code of procedure. Their habit of mind, their attitude toward their profession, have been profoundly influenced by it. To sweep away the habits and methods patiently acquired through a long period of training and experience, and substitute for it an entirely new system, is a real hardship, and involves, temporarily at least, serious inconvenience in the administration of the law. There is always the danger that a liberal system will be rendered narrow and technical by code-trained lawyers, and unfortunately those most competent to aid in reform are those who, because of professional obligations, are least able to give it their assistance. "Better endure the evils we know than fly to those we know not of," is the attitude of most lawyers; but it is a choice of evils which confronts us, and the hopelessness of ever remedying the evils of our code under existing conditions should nerve us to undertake to effect a remedy by a change of method which is scientifically adapted to the end to be accomplished. We all owe something to posterity, and lawyers owe a debt to their own profession, obligations on which a large credit would be given if a systematic and sustained effort were made toward accomplishing an intelligent reform of procedure.

In the discussion of the general aspects of the subject, we have refrained, for want of time, from dealing with specific branches of procedure for which there is urgent need of reform, regardless of the system adopted. Among these, however, might be mentioned, in passing, the reform of the law of evidence, particularly with reference to the proof of books of account, reform in the method of the proof of sanity, or insanity, by expert testimony, reform of the rule as to the legal effect to be given to insanity in homicide cases, the reform in procedure both before and after judgment in actions brought to recover debt, reform in the methods of selecting a jury, especially in cases of wide public interest.

A matter to which serious attention should be directed is the double appeal. In a large number of cases in this and a number of other states two appeals may be had as a matter of right. The absurdity, as well as the inconvenience, of such a procedure is obvious. Assuming that an appellate bench is competent to bear the responsibilities placed upon it, there is no sound reason why in the ordinary case suitors should suffer the inconvenience, expense, and delay of having their cases twice argued on appeal on the same record. The present system inevitably results in every case of importance, being twice appealed where that right exists, and the first appeal is more than likely to be dealt with in a perfunctory manner by a court which knows that its own decision will not be final. Either there should be one appellate court with a sufficient number of judges to hear and formally dispose of all appeals taken to it direct from the trial court, or the intermediate appellate court, corresponding to our own Appellate Division of the Supreme Court, should be the final court of appeal, except in those cases where because of public interest, or to settle doubtful points of law, an appeal is allowed either by the intermediate court or by the court of last resort.

Some of these questions will undoubtedly receive the attention of the Constitutional Convention to be held in this state next month. But all of them are of slight importance as compared with the larger problem of securing as a substitute for our present Code of Civil Procedure a system which shall conform to the three fundamental principles of a sound procedure; namely, avoidance of the attempt to regulate minutely every step in practice, free scope for judicial discretion, and freedom from irresponsible and bungling amendment.

VI

CONSTITUTIONAL LIMITATIONS

By a constitution we mean the body of legal rules or precepts which regulate or control governmental action. We commonly think of a constitution as a written instrument like our own Constitution; but it need not be written. A constitution may exist in the form of unwritten rules or precepts, provided there is some organization in the state which will compel their observance; and in the case of some of the European states, we speak of those rules and precepts which morally and practically affect the control of the government as its Constitution, although there exists no formal organization or agency for compelling obedience to those rules.

Whether written or unwritten, a constitution is the will expressed in law of the ultimate sovereignty of the state. This becomes evident in countries like the United States, where the constitution-making body is distinct from the ordinary legislative body. In the United States Congress is the legislative body, but it can only act in the way and to the extent permitted by the Constitution. The constitution-making body which makes and amends the Constitution which is imposed not only on Congress, but on the executive and judicial branches of the government both state and national, is the Constitutional Convention, which under Article V of the Constitution is composed of the legislatures or constitutional conventions of the several states, three-fourths of which must concur in order to amend the Constitution. Thus the several legislatures or constitutional conventions of the several states acting together as a constitutional convention constitute the supreme law-making body of the state, and its enactments may legally limit the power and control the action of all the legislative bodies in the country and all other agencies of government. In England the Constitution is unwritten, and the constitution-making body is Parliament, which is also the ordinary legislative body. In fact, I think it may be said that the House of Commons is the constitution-making body, since it has demonstrated, especially in its recent history, its power to impose its own limitations on all governmental agencies, including the House of Lords.

The sole object and purpose of a constitution should be to give stability to government and to protect individuals from oppression, both by the established agencies of government and by temporary majorities which may control some branch of the government. Since a constitution emanates from the ultimate authority of the state organized in its constitution-making body, it expresses merely the ultimate will of the state, and cannot permanently, or indeed for any considerable period of time, run counter to its wishes. In theory constitutions are brought into harmony with the popular will by the process of amendment, but amendments to constitutions are usually attended by sufficient difficulty to insure deliberation and careful consideration on the part of the body politic before making them effective.

In its last analysis, therefore, a constitution is nothing more or less than a check on the arbitrary and oppressive exercise of governmental power, which cannot be hastily set aside or overturned, and which cannot be affected by the clamor or the action of mere temporary majorities.

A citizen in any one of the United States is subject to two constitutions: the Constitution of the United States and the constitution of the state in which he resides. The Constitution of the United States was adopted by the Constitutional Convention called together by Congress in 1787. The Constitution adopted by the Convention was, pursuant to its provisions, ratified by eleven states, and went into effect as between them in 1789. The state of North Carolina ratified the Constitution later in the year, and the state of Rhode Island ratified the Constitution the following year, thus bringing within its control all of the thirteen original colonial states.

Most of the thirteen original states organized and adopted constitutions during the Revolution before any steps were taken to establish the Federal Constitution or the Articles of Confederation which preceded the Constitution. Connecticut and Rhode Island alone continued their government under the form of their colonial charters. Massachusetts adopted a constitution which was ratified by its people and which has continued in force down to the present time, subject, of course, to amendment from time to time.

All of the states now have written constitutions which have been more or less completely revised from time to time. Texas, for example, has had seven constitutions, and Kansas has had three constitutions in as many years. The Colony of New York adopted its first constitution in 1777. A second constitution was adopted in 1821, and a third in 1846; and the present constitution now undergoing complete revision by the Constitutional Convention was adopted in 1894.

The Federal Constitution provides for its amendment in Article V, which in part reads as follows:

> The Congress, whenever two-thirds of both Houses shall deem it necessary, shall propose Amendments to this Constitution, or, on the Application of the Legislatures of two-thirds of the several States, shall call a Convention for proposing Amendments, which, in either case, shall be valid to all Intents and Purposes, as Part of this Constitution, when ratified by the Legislatures of three-fourths of the several States, or by Conventions in three-fourths thereof, as the one or the other Mode of Ratification may be proposed by the Congress; Provided . . . that no State, without its consent, shall be deprived of its equal Suffrage in the Senate.

All of the state constitutions contain provisions for their amendment; usually by state conventions, whose acts are submitted for ratification by popular vote, or by legislative acts, which must be submitted to the people and approved by popular vote before they are adopted as amendments.

Under the present Constitution of New York it is provided that amendments may be proposed by vote of a majority of the members of the Senate and Assembly if approved by a majority of the members in the next succeeding Senate and Assembly. The amendment is then submitted to the people, and if approved by a majority of the electors voting upon the amendment, it then becomes a part of the Constitution. Provision is also made for the calling of a constitutional convention to be authorized by popular vote in the year 1916 and every twentieth year thereafter, and also at such times as the Legislature may by law provide. The convention is composed of delegates elected, three each, from each of the Senatorial Districts of the state. Amendments adopted by this convention must be submitted to popular vote for ratification.

The main objects sought to be effected by the Federal Constitution may be roughly classified as follows: first, the organization of the Federal government into three great departments, the executive, the legislative, and the judicial, which, in theory, at least, are independent, each of the others, and each of which must be limited to its own sphere; second, the separation and distribution of powers of government between the Federal government and the state governments. The Federal government, under the Constitution, became a government of delegated powers, and powers not expressly delegated to it by the states or granted by fair implication from powers expressly granted are reserved to the states; third, the limitation by the express provisions of the Constitution of the powers of the legislative bodies of both Federal and state governments to pass laws interfering with those fundamental personal rights which have been believed by English-speaking peoples to be essential to the liberty and happiness of a free people.

The scope of the state constitutions is necessarily

more limited, since the relation of state and Federal governments is fixed by the Federal Constitution. The function of the state constitutions is limited to the organization of the state governments into executive, legislative, and judicial departments, and in limiting the powers of the agencies of the state governments to encroach on personal rights. Thus the citizens of every state are subject to a dual constitutional system, each supreme in its own sphere, the state constitution being limited in its operation to the territory of the particular state, whereas the Federal Constitution is operative in all the states. This would doubtless be implied by the character of the government created by the dual system, but the Federal Constitution, Article VI, expressly provides:

> This Constitution, and the Laws of the United States which shall be made in Pursuance thereof; and all Treaties made, or which shall be made, under the Authority of the United States, shall be the Supreme Law of the Land; and the Judges in every State shall be bound thereby, and any Thing in the Constitution or laws of any State to the Contrary notwithstanding.

Assuming that under this system any branch of the government, for example, the legislative, state or national, oversteps the limits imposed upon it by the Constitution, who is to determine whether or not the act of the legislature is constitutional? Under the European systems of constitutional government no branch of the government is deemed to have the power to pass upon the constitutionality of the acts of any other branch of the government. The result is that in this respect those constitutions are not, for all purposes, true legal limitations upon the powers of the government, but are rather, in the last analysis, moral precepts, or powerful influences, upon the sentiment of those charged with the responsibility of government, but without any legal or judicial sanction in the sense that there resides in any official or agency of government the power to compel obedience to constitutional provisions.

The Federal Constitution contains no provisions specifically giving to the courts power to declare statutes unconstitutional. In the famous case of Marbury against Madison, decided by the Supreme Court in 1803, the opinion being written by the great Chief Justice John Marshall, it was held that the Court had the power to declare an act of Congress unconstitutional if, in the judgment of the Court, it conflicted with any provision of the Constitution.

By Article III, Section 2 of the Constitution, the Supreme Court was given original jurisdiction in cases affecting ambassadors, public ministers, and those in which a state should be a party. "In all other cases" the court was given appellate jurisdiction. A statute was passed by Congress purporting to give to the court original jurisdiction to issue the common law writ of mandamus, the purpose of which was to compel the officers of the government to perform administrative or ministerial duties. A commission appointing Marbury a justice of the peace in the District of Columbia having been duly executed and James Madison, then Secretary of State, having refused to deliver the commission, Marbury brought an original proceeding in the Supreme Court for a mandamus compelling Madison, as Secretary of State, to deliver the commission.

By endeavoring to give to the court powers not conferred upon it by the Constitution the statute enacted by Congress came into direct conflict with the express provisions of the Constitution, which provided that "in all other cases" except those specified in the Constitution the court should have appellate jurisdiction. The court held that it was its constitutional duty to disregard an act of Congress which was inconsistent with the Constitution; that its judges were sworn to uphold the Constitution, which was, by Article VI, made the supreme law of the land; that all acts of Congress were subject to and inferior in authority to the Constitution, and when in conflict with it, it was the duty of the court to disregard the inferior enactment.

It is a matter of some interest that in rendering this decision the court was invoking the Constitution in denying to itself powers which Congress had sought, contrary to the Constitution, to confer upon it. Another point to be noted is that the court did not directly interfere with the machinery of a coördinate branch of the government. It merely refused to allow its own machinery to be used to give sanction to a statute which in its judgment conflicted with the Constitution by which it was bound. The doctrine of Marbury against Madison was held in later decisions for like reasons to apply in the case of laws passed by states in conflict with the Federal Constitution, and state courts have been unanimously held to possess like powers, both under the Federal Constitution and the several state constitutions.

A study of the Federal Constitution and the conditions leading to its enactment seems to leave no reasonable doubt that the doctrine of Marbury against Madison is logically and historically sound, and that the result of that decision was precisely that intended by the framers of the Constitution.

The governments of the several colonies were organized under royal charters defining the powers of the colonial government. If legislation enacted by the colonial legislatures did not conform to their respective charters, such legislation was void and could be held to be void by the colonial courts or by the English courts on appeal. The legal notion, therefore, that legislation could be made inferior to a higher and authoritative grant of legislative powers, and could be determined to be such by the courts, was not a new one.

Following the outbreak of the Revolution the several state constitutions which were then adopted were practically substitutes for the colonial grants or charters, and the courts in New York, New Jersey, and Rhode Island prior to 1787 not unnaturally decided that they possessed the power to declare acts of the legislature unconstitutional and void, if in conflict with their respective constitutions. Thus when the Constitutional Convention met in 1787, the theory of judicial power to declare legislation unconstitutional must have been one well understood by most of the members of the Convention. That the Federal Constitution was understood to confer such powers on the courts is indicated by the discussions of the time, notably in the writings of Alexander Hamilton, in the *Federalist*, in Chancellor Kent's lectures; and in the case of Marbury against Madison, no serious question seems to have been raised as to the intention of the framers to confer this power upon the courts.

There was, however, a more fundamental reason than mere historical precedent, why the framers of the Constitution should have reserved to the courts the power to pass upon the constitutionality of acts of the legislature, both state and national. For the first time constitutional provision was being made for a dual form of government exercising authority over the same territory, each supreme within its own sphere. It therefore became essential that the power to determine the limitations on the authority of each government should either be conferred upon some judicial body or be left to the arbitrament of force through conflict of the agencies of the respective governments. Not without its effect, also, was the lively impression made upon the minds of the publicists of the time and upon popular opinion, of the dangers to individual liberty, from the arbitrary exercise of legislative and governmental power. This was not only a direct inheritance of the colonists from English history, but was the most potent influence affecting the popular imagination during the revolutionary period. To have formulated in written language a separation of governmental powers into state and national with specific limitations upon each, as the supreme law of the land, and to have denied to the courts the power to apply that law in the settlement of controversies pending before them, would have been not only contrary to the experience of the colonies, but would have involved the performance of the functions of government in confusion and in conflicts of authority which would have imperiled the success of the great experiment.

All these possibilities were avoided by making the Constitution the supreme law of the land and leaving its interpretation to the courts, which are thus authorized to determine, in controversies brought before them, whether legislation is in conflict with the provisions of the Constitution and thus legally inoperative. By vesting this power ultimately in the Supreme Court, a body removed from political activity and possessing no control over the armed forces or material resources of the nation, and by the method of its constitution removed from the immediate pressure of popular clamor, the Constitution insured the peace and order of the country and intrusted the civil liberty of its citizens to the body best adapted to preserve and perpetuate it.

The most enlightened thinkers of the day urge upon the world the submission of international controversies and the interpretation of treaties to a permanent judicial tribunal, as a substitute for the arbitrament of arms. It would be a strange anomaly if at this day the settlement of differences between our two systems of government should be withdrawn from our Supreme Court and either left unsettled or settled according to arbitrary determination of the agencies of the respective governments.

In discussing the question whether the courts should have the power to declare legislation unconstitutional, it should be remembered that that power under our system is purely judicial in character, a principle which has been adopted by the Federal courts under the Federal Constitution and by the state courts under both the Federal Constitution and the various state constitutions. The courts determine the constitutionality of statutes only when the question is directly brought before them by litigation. They do not have power to pass upon legislative acts concerning purely political questions, nor do they possess the power to interfere directly with the action of either of the other departments of the government, the legislative and executive.

There is no constitutional authority in the United States Supreme Court to act in an advisory capacity to other departments of the government, but in some of the states, notably Massachusetts, there is constitutional authority for such action by the courts. Opinions thus given are deemed to be advisory only, and consequently do not constitute precedents.

The power of courts to determine legislative acts unconstitutional is often referred to as being peculiar to our own system. As a matter of fact, the constitutions of Australia, New Zealand, and the British North America Acts (regulating the government of Canada), contain provisions not only recognizing the power of the judiciary to pass upon the constitutionality of legislative acts, but provide that executive and legislative may in certain cases procure the opinion of the judiciary as to specified constitutional questions. It is interesting to note, however, that the Constitutional Convention of Australia, held in 1900, long before the agitation for the recall of judicial decisions in the United States, rejected the proposition for the adoption of the recall of judicial decisions, and adopted provisions authorizing the judiciary to pass upon the constitutionality and therefore the validity of legislation.

As originally adopted, the only limitation upon the powers of the Federal government to encroach upon private civil rights was that contained in Article I, Section 9, which prohibited the suspension of the right of *habeas corpus* except in case of rebellion or invasion, and prohibited bills of attainder and *ex post facto* laws. The feeling was widespread that the Constitution as adopted by the Convention did not adequately protect private rights, and its final acceptance by the thirteen states was induced in part, at least, by the promise that amendments would be added, insuring to citizens of the new government the protection of an adequate bill of rights. In 1791 the first ten amendments to the Federal Constitution were adopted. These amendments were limitations on the powers of the Federal government only and had no force so far as the legislation of the several states was concerned. Without enumerating them in detail, it is sufficient to say that they guaranteed, so far as the Federal government was concerned, those fundamental rights which were deemed to be the natural inheritance of the English colonists and which had already been incorporated into the constitutions of the several states. The more important of these were freedom of religious worship, the right peaceably to assemble, the right to bear arms, the right to be free from unreasonable searches and seizures, the right to a speedy trial by jury, the right not to be compelled to testify against oneself in a criminal trial, the right not to be deprived of life, liberty, or property without due process of law, and the like.

Prior to 1865 the limitations of the Federal Constitution on the powers of state government were mainly directed toward the organization of the dual governments and the proper separation of their powers, as, for example, the prohibition of the states from entering into treaty relations with foreign governments, the coining of money, the laying of impost duties on imports or exports. The powers of the state were also limited indirectly by the various powers delegated to the Federal government under the Constitution, as is notably the case in power given to Congress to regulate commerce between the several states and with foreign countries. The only direct limitation on the powers of the states to encroach upon the private rights of their own citizens was the provision contained in Article I, Section 10, that "No state shall . . . pass any bill of attainder, *ex post facto* law or law impairing the obligation of contract."

This provision was broadly interpreted by the courts, and in substance prevented the adoption of any law either by legislation or judicial decision which created or changed adversely any punishment for crime after the criminal act sought to be punished, and in a similar way it prohibited the adoption of any law impairing the obligation and therefore the rights arising under preëxisting contracts — and the word *contracts* was broadly interpreted so as to include not only technical contracts, but deeds, grants, and charters, the principle which was established in the famous Dartmouth College case. There was also an indirect limitation under Article IV, Section 2 of the Constitution, which provided that citizens of each state should be entitled to all the privileges and immunities of citizens in the several states. The practical effect of this provision was that a citizen of one state going to another state could not in the second state be subjected to laws which discriminated against him as a citizen of the first.

In 1865 the Thirteenth Amendment was adopted, providing that slavery should not exist in the United States nor in any place subject to its jurisdiction. This was followed in 1868 by the adoption of the Fourteenth Amendment, which, in our day, has given rise to more litigation and more discussion than practically all of the other provisions of the Constitution taken together. This amendment first defined citizenship in the United States by declaring that all persons born or naturalized in the United States and subject to the jurisdiction thereof are citizens of the United States and of the state in which they reside. The amendment then provided as follows: "No state shall make or enforce any law which shall abridge the privileges or immunities of citizens of the United States, nor shall any state deprive any person of life, liberty or property without due process of law, nor deny to any person within its jurisdiction the equal protection of the laws."

The obvious purpose of the amendment was to limit directly the power of the states to impair or interfere with the immunities and privileges of citizens of the United States and to protect what were believed to be fundamental rights of all persons to life, liberty, and property from unjust encroachment by the several states, and to insure to all persons within the state the equal protection of its laws. While this is the general purport of the amendment, its language is somewhat vague and indefinite, and it may well be doubted whether the supporters of the amendment had in mind precisely the kind of governmental encroachments which were intended to be prohibited. In any event, they wisely avoided any attempt at detailed enumeration or definition of them. It was therefore left to the courts to give to the amendment its meaning and vitality.

Overmuch attention has been given by some writers and critics of the judicial interpretation of the amendment to the fact that the immediate occasion for the passage of the Fourteenth Amendment was the necessity of protecting the slaves lately freed by the Thirteenth Amendment from unjust and discriminatory legislation of the states. Whatever the immediate occasion and purpose of the amendment, it is hardly to be supposed that language so general and unrestricted as that incorporated into our governmental charter should be limited in its interpretation by such considerations, or that rights and immunities guaranteed to the negro by its provisions could not be availed of by the white man should occasion arise.

The privileges and immunities of citizens of the United States which are protected by the Fourteenth Amendment have been declared by the courts to be those privileges and immunities which inhere in the citizen by virtue of the Constitution and laws of the United States, as the right to engage in interstate and foreign commerce; the right to invoke the protection of the Federal government or to resort to its courts. As thus interpreted, this phrase did not have the extensive effect given to the phrases immediately following, which prohibited any state from depriving any person of life, liberty, or property without due process of law, or from denying to any person within its jurisdiction equal protection of the laws. And it is under these latter clauses that the serious questions as to the extent of the power of the courts to declare laws unconstitutional have arisen.

The phrase "due process of law" has been construed to mean not only due or reasonable procedure where there is a deprivation of life, liberty, or property by process of law, but the courts have also held that the so-called fundamental rights of person and property cannot be taken in certain cases by process of law, however orderly the procedure adopted. Thus there may be a failure of due process when the procedure by which life, liberty, or property is taken is unreasonable, harsh, or arbitrary, although if a proper procedure were adopted, there would be no constitutional prohibition of the end sought to be attained. On the other hand, whatever the procedure adopted, there can be no arbitrary interference with life, liberty, or property by state action. It is beyond the scope of this discussion to attempt to define with precision or comprehensively the phrase "due process of law" as applied to procedure. In general, however, it may be said that the power of taking life, liberty, or property when lawful as a substantive right must be exercised by an official or body having jurisdiction over the subject-matter, and that reasonable notice of the proceeding or governmental act must be given, and opportunity for a fair hearing must be afforded.

Established procedure recognized and accepted at common law or before the adoption of the Constitution is "due process" in a procedural sense, but it does not follow that a new form of procedure is not due process. Thus, it has been held that a state may regulate or even abolish trial by jury if some reasonable method of trial is substituted for it, and that prosecution for crime by indictment may be constitutionally abolished, and prosecution by information lodged with a magistrate substituted for it. Nor do the provisions of the constitutions protect one from the operation of a state law requiring one charged with crime to testify against himself.

What is a reasonable notice or fair hearing, of course, varies widely with the circumstances of each case. The summary taking of property by administrative officers and boards authorized by statutes to carry out the administration of police powers and the powers of taxation have generally been upheld. Thus, the summary action of boards of health, the summary seizing of game unlawfully possessed during the closed season, or of articles possessed for illegal purposes has been upheld. On the other hand, if provisions of statute deprive citizens from access to the courts or unduly hinder such access, or if the courts themselves, through corruption, fraud, or duress, do not render an honest decision, there is a denial of due process of law.

Liberty, as used in the Fourteenth Amendment, means more than liberty of person. As has been said by the Supreme Court,

> The term is deemed to embrace the right of the citizen to be free in the enjoyment of all his faculties; to be free to use them in lawful ways; to live and work where he will; to earn his livelihood by any lawful calling; to pursue any livelihood or association,

and for that purpose to enter into all contracts which may be proper, necessary or essential to his carrying to a successful conclusion the purposes above mentioned.

By deprivation of property is meant not alone the appropriation of property by action of a state, but such limitations upon its use and enjoyment as amount in some substantial manner to an interference with or loss of the beneficial use by the owner. Since the so-called rights of property, as we have already pointed out, are essentially personal rights, and are essential to personal liberty, there is, in many cases, no clear line of demarcation between acts which are unconstitutional because they deprive of personal liberty and those which deprive of property.

The meaning of the phrase "equal protection of the laws," is self-evident. It does not mean, however, that every person in the community must be subject to the same laws, or under the law may exercise the same rights and privileges. The single trade, business, or profession may be regulated by legislation, and those engaging in them respectively may be given special rights and privileges and be subject to special restrictions. A physician or a lawyer may be subject to lawful restrictions not imposed on business men or clergymen. In other words, there may be constitutional discrimination in legislation provided the legislation serves a public purpose and the discrimination has a just and reasonable basis. If the discrimination is arbitrary and unreasonable, not based upon a legitimate governmental purpose, then it denies the equal protection of the laws guaranteed by the Fourteenth Amendment.

As thus construed by the courts, the Fourteenth

Amendment has been a powerful and efficient agency in the protection of civil liberty from the encroachment of state governmental action and from the injustice of special and class legislation, and it has been justly regarded by many political and legal thinkers as marking the great advance during the nineteenth century in the protection of civil rights. Under its protection it has been held, for example, that the conviction of a negro of crime by a jury from which all members of his race were excluded by statute or by the arbitrary exercise of judicial power was unconstitutional, because it denied due process of law; and that the taking of property for a private purpose or for public purposes without just compensation is not due process of law. Regulation of rates of public service companies which is confiscatory is the taking of property without due process of law, and unconstitutional. A state court has no power to render personal judgment against a defendant who is not brought within the jurisdiction of the court within that state. The denial of the right to resort to the courts under the Constitution and laws of the United States, or the imposition of penalties for so doing are unconstitutional, because they deny due process of law.

As corporations are the creatures of the state, they possess no rights except such as are conferred by the state. The Fourteenth Amendment, therefore, affords very little protection to corporations. The Supreme Court has held that a corporation is not a "citizen" within the meaning of Article IV, Section 2 of the Constitution, which provides that citizens of each state shall be entitled to all the privileges and immunities of citizens in the several states, and that therefore this provision affords no protection to corporations as citizens of a state. Corporations engaged in interstate commerce are subject to the provisions of the Constitution, reserving to the Federal government the right to regulate commerce, and under the decision in the Dartmouth College case, a corporate charter is a contract which may not be impaired by state action. Very generally, now, however, states in granting corporate charters reserve the right to amend or repeal them, subject to these limitations. Therefore, a state may determine absolutely the terms upon which a corporation may be created or may do business within its limits, or may exclude it from doing business within the state altogether, unless such state action amounts to an interference with the power reserved to the Federal government to regulate commerce.

The prohibitions of the Fourteenth Amendment obviously cannot be deemed to restrict the power of government to make proper regulations for the protection of the health, safety, and morals of its citizens, even though such regulations involve to some extent limitations on liberty and the use of property by individuals. To do so would amount to a deprivation of government of those powers which are essential to the order and well-being of civilized communities. This power of regulation, for want of a better name, has been termed the police power, and the courts have held that the Fourteenth Amendment is no limitation upon the proper exercise of the police power of the state governments. No attempt has been made by the Supreme Court to define the exact limits of the police power, but certain classes of legislation may now be said to fall definitely within its limits. Thus, reasonable regulations to protect or promote the public health, even though they interfere with the liberty of individuals or the free use of property, are a proper exercise of the police power, and constitutional. Thus, a state may make regulations to insure the purity and healthfulness of food sold within it. It may reasonably limit the hours of labor in unhealthful occupations, as in underground mines, and a law prohibiting the employment of women in public laundries for more than ten hours a day has been upheld as constitutional. In the same way, reasonable regulation affecting the public morals, public safety, and public order are all within the police powers of a state. Thus, the regulation or suppression of the liquor traffic, gambling, lotteries, immoral practices, the regulation of railroads, construction work and street traffic, for purposes of public safety, are familiar examples of the exercise of the police power which are constitutional, notwithstanding the fact that they may interfere to some extent with the liberty or property of individuals.

Where, however, legislatures have enacted regulations affecting the economic welfare of the state, the tendency of the courts has been to restrict this power to narrow limits, where such legislation interferes with individual liberty or private property. Thus, limitations of the hours of labor, except where the public health or morals is concerned, has been held unconstitutional, as has also legislation forbidding the arbitrary refusal to employ workmen because they were members of labor unions. On the other hand, reasonable legislative control of business affected with a public interest, that is to say, business essentially governmental in character or requiring public franchises, or which constitutes a natural monopoly, has been upheld. Thus, the constitutional power to regulate all so-called public service corporations, as public carriers, public grain elevators, telephone companies, gas and electric companies, has been definitely established.

A still wider scope for governmental action under the Fourteenth Amendment is now claimed in behalf of the various types of workmen's compensation acts. This now offers a great field for judicial controversy under the Constitution. There seems to be little doubt that a proper scheme for workmen's compensation for injuries received by employees, at least in those trades which are inherently dangerous, is economically desirable, and it seems highly probable that workmen's compensation acts, made applicable to dangerous trades or under the provisions of which the common-law rights of employer and employee may be preserved if the parties so stipulate upon beginning the employment, will be held to be constitutional. Whether, however, such laws arbitrarily imposing the liability to pay workmen's compensation to the employee in all classes of employment regardless of the employer's fault and regardless of his common-law liability transgress the constitutional prohibition against taking property without due process of law, is a question which still remains to be definitely answered by the Supreme Court.

In the now celebrated Ives case the Court of Appeals of New York, a court of unquestioned integrity and of great learning and ability, held that such legislation violated the Fourteenth Amendment and the similar provisions of the Constitution of the State of New York. Without attempting any extended analysis of this decision, it may be said that the substance of it was that the workmen's compensation statute, when applied, did deprive the employer of property without any common-law liability on his part, and the mere fact that the deprivation in the cases provided for by statute was economically desirable, did not constitute the taking due process of law. In reaching this result, the court was strongly influenced by the argument that for the court to hold in effect that legislation which authorized the taking of private property of one class to bestow it on another class, because of supposed economic benefits, was constitutional, would sweep away all the constitutional guarantees of the Fourteenth Amendment, so far as they related to the taking of property. As was said by the Court:

> The right of property rests not upon philosophical or scientific speculations nor upon the commendable impulses of benevolence or charity, nor yet upon the dictates of natural justice. The right has its foundation in the fundamental law. That can be changed by the people, not by legislatures. In a government like ours theories of public good or necessity are often so plausible or sound as to command popular approval, but courts are not permitted to forget that the law is the only chart by which the ship of state is to be guided. Law as used in this sense means the basic law and not the very act of legislation which deprives the citizen of his rights, privileges, or property. Any other view would lead to the absurdity that the Constitutions protect only those rights which the legislatures do not take away. If such economic and sociologic arguments as are here advanced in support of this statute can be allowed to subvert the fundamental idea of property, then there is no private right entirely safe, because there is no limitation upon the absolute discretion of legislatures, and the guarantees of the Con-

stitutions are a mere waste of words. (Ives *v.* South Buffalo Ry. Co., 201 N. Y. 271, at p. 294.)

This language may well commend itself to the thoughtful, and lead to the conclusion that the proper method of securing the economic benefits of workmen's compensation, if such legislation is to go beyond the limits above indicated, is "by the orderly process of constitutional amendment rather than by making a universal test of the right to take private property for the supposed economic advantage to result therefrom."

The decision in the Ives case was the occasion of an outburst of criticism of the Court of Appeals, so loud, so ill-tempered, and so misguided, as to startle those who have respect for and faith in our institutions. At best the question involved was a debatable one and was so regarded by the competent lawyers who had prepared the workmen's compensation act, and had upheld its constitutionality before the courts. Concededly, a decision in favor of the legislation would have extended widely the known boundaries of the police power of the states. The effect of the decision actually rendered was to open the way for the establishment of workmen's compensation by constitutional amendment so framed as to preserve the more fundamental constitutional guarantees. The spirit which under such circumstances dictated virulent attacks upon the court by the unsuccessful litigants is a spirit essentially lawless and subversive of all orderly judicial procedure.

So far as these attacks have given rise to any philosophic criticism worthy of the serious consideration of students of law and of our constitutional system, it is expressed in the phrase "social justice" and the claim that the courts, in determining the constitutionality of legislation under the Fourteenth Amendment, have failed to recognize and apply the principle of "social justice." As already pointed out in an earlier lecture, the phrase itself, as stating any definite legal conception, is meaningless. The idea, however, which it is intended to express is, I believe, that in passing upon the constitutionality of so-called social legislation, the courts should accept as conclusive the opinion of the legislature as to the economic desirability of the statute, and thus not assume to declare the legislation unconstitutional if it seeks in good faith to carry into effect economic reform which, in the opinion of the legislature, is desirable. The only other alternative, of course, would be for the court to act upon its own opinion of what constitutes social and economic welfare, unguided by precedent, the difficulties of which have been referred to in an earlier chapter.

From our discussion of the subject, it will not have escaped your attention that under our existing law when the court passes upon the constitutionality of state legislation under the Fourteenth Amendment, there are three main propositions involved. First, as was determined in Marbury against Madison, and as has ever since been the law, the power to determine the constitutionality of the statute is vested in the court by the Constitution. Second, assuming that the statute involves the deprivation of property or liberty, whether the statute in its scope is within the police power of the state, and therefore not prohibited by the Constitution, and finally, assuming that the statute is within the scope of the police power, whether its purposes are carried out in a reasonable and proper manner. The first two questions are, of course, questions of law; the third is largely a question of fact. Thus in the case of the workmen's compensation statutes, the court must determine whether the statutes taking the property of the employer for workmen's compensation for the purpose of working public benefit exclusively economic in character are within the police power and whether the particular statute adopted is a reasonable and proper exercise of that power. That under our system it is the sworn duty of the court to determine these questions in accordance with its own best judgment, rather than adopt the judgment of the legislature or what it may conceive to be the popular judgment, is not now open to question.

Beginning with Marbury against Madison, and following through the long line of judicial decisions, both in the Federal and the state courts, one may trace step by step the development and establishment of the doctrine of judicial power to pass upon the constitutionality of legislative acts. I have already referred to the view that the constitution conferred and was intended to confer this power on the judiciary as logically and historically sound, and this view has now been accepted and acted upon not only judicially but politically for a hundred years.

If the requirement of "social justice," therefore, be that the courts should accept as conclusive or in any sense controlling the opinion of the legislature as to what is a proper exercise of the police power in social legislation, this requirement can be met only by a change in the structure of our law by constitutional amendment; that is to say, it is now primarily a political instead of a legal question, and we shall make very little progress toward its proper solution by calling the court names because its view of what is a proper exercise of the police power does not coincide with our own.

Since the decision in the Ives case, the constitution of the state of New York has been amended by the adoption of a provision expressly authorizing the passage of a workmen's compensation act. Thus, by the orderly process of the law the supreme law of the state has been brought into harmony with the popular will, and a complete scheme of workmen's compensation is now in operation in this state. Whether this law will be upheld by the Supreme Court remains to be seen; but the history of the subject in New York emphasizes the fact that there is a direct and orderly method of correcting the erroneous determination of courts if such are made, and of bringing the provisions of our Constitution into harmony with the popular will without resorting to ill-tempered abuse of the courts.

The recall of decisions is a suggested method of accomplishing this result. The recall of decisions, properly understood, is nothing more or less than a method of amending the constitution by popular vote. Its proposal was based on the false assumption that amendment of the constitution by existing constitutional methods was extremely difficult or impossible. Since the proposal of recall of decisions, the constitution of the state of New York, as we have already seen, has been amended so as to authorize workmen's compensation without undue delay or inconvenience, and two amendments to the Federal Constitution have been adopted.

Other objections to the process of constitutional amendment by judicial recall will readily occur to the student of constitutional law. In so far as it is a more speedy method of amending the Constitution, it tends to remove the main distinction between constitutional provisions and ordinary legislation. Both the constitution and legislation represent the popular will. A constitution is merely a check on legislation in so far only as it requires time and deliberation before the check can be removed. Its value consists in the protection which it affords to private rights in the first instance, and in the certainty that that protection cannot be removed by temporary majorities or without the deliberate and mature consideration which tends to remove popular passion and prejudice from the settlement of political questions. If constitutional limitations may be removed by popular vote whenever and immediately they are found by the courts to conflict with popular legislation, all those dangers are invited which the framers of the Constitution hoped to avoid by the adoption of a written constitution.

The recall of decisions as a method of constitutional amendment, moreover, presents technical difficulties which would give rise to no little confusion in practice. By the recall of a decision, all that would be ascertained by any given recall would be that the statute determined by the court to be unconstitutional was by the recall determined to be constitutional. Whether constitutional in whole or in part, what reasons should be assigned for the recall, what judicial principle established, or whether the principle should be extended to other classes of cases, are questions which must remain unanswered by the recall. In other words, it is an attempt to establish a constitutional rule for judicial guidance by popular vote, without announcing what the rule is either in form or substance. We thus amend our constitution without indicating the scope of the amendment and leave it to the courts and legislature to guess what class of legislative acts may be lawfully enacted.

Whether "social justice" should be adopted as a principle of constitutional interpretation by the courts need not be discussed further than it has already been discussed in our consideration of judicial precedent and the power of the courts to declare legislation unconstitutional. The extent to which, in the criticism of courts accompanying much of the public discussion of this subject, all sense of proportion has been lost is disclosed by a writer in the Columbia Law Review, on "The Progressiveness of the United States Supreme Court."

He shows that during the twenty-five years from 1887 to 1912, the United States Supreme Court rendered 560 decisions involving the validity of state statutes, under the Federal Constitution, and that in the case of all these decisions, except three, the United States Supreme Court sustained the validity of the state legislation, including labor legislation, anti-trust legislation, liquor and cigarette legislation, pure food legislation, regulation of railways, and other corporation laws involving the freedom of contract, etc.

The situation is therefore obviously not one to inspire any serious apprehension of the oppressive exercise of the judicial power of the Supreme Court to declare statutes unconstitutional, or calling for any radical overturning of our constitutional system. The power to restrict and control governmental action must be lodged somewhere. Under our system it is lodged with the Constitutional Convention, representing the whole people. As the whole people cannot continuously speak through a Constitutional Convention, it is necessary to delegate that power to some body or agency. With us it is delegated to the Supreme Court, under the guidance of a written constitution. The alternative is to leave it to be controlled by the decision of temporary majorities of each legislative body in the country, affected as they may be and often are by temporary or local influences. Notwithstanding any passing dissatisfaction we may feel at the particular decision of a court as to the constitutionality of a statute, is there after all any body in our governmental scheme which is, judged in the light of experience, by the method of its selection and its freedom from untoward influences, better qualified to exercise this power, or to whom it may be more safely intrusted than the judiciary?

VII

BENCH AND BAR

Burke, in his celebrated oration for conciliation with the Colonies, referred to the spirit and activity of the lawyer class in the American Colonies as one of the capital causes of the spirit of liberty in the New World. "In no country, perhaps, in the world," he said, "is the law so generally studied," and in proof of this statement he referred to the great number of lawyers who were members of the Continental Congress; to the fact that law books were being printed in the Colonies for their own use; and that as many of Blackstone's "Commentaries" had been sold in America as in England. He expressed the opinion that it was the widespread study of and interest in law which made the colonists so "acute, inquisitive, dextrous, prompt in attack, ready in defense, full of resources"; which led them "to augur misgovernment at a distance and snuff the approach of tyranny in every tainted breeze."

Burke's picture of the legal profession in the Colonies during the Revolution, and of its influences on public opinion, was not overdrawn.

The record of the legal profession during the Revolutionary period will always remain one of the bright pages of American history. Such names as James Otis, John Adams, Josiah Quincy, Robert Paine, of Massachusetts; Peyton Randolph, Patrick Henry, Edmund Pendleton, of Virginia; Charles Carroll and Samuel Chase, of Maryland; Alexander Hamilton and James Kent, of New York, at once recall to memory the leadership and influence of the bar during the American Revolution. Lawyers were the most influential members of the Colonial legislatures and of the Continental Congress. Of the fifty-five signers of the Declaration of Independence more than half were lawyers. They kindled the flame of the Revolution in the Colonies; they translated the Revolution into institutions under the forms of law with a skill and a statesmanlike grasp which has excited the wonder and admiration of the historian.

The profession had brought with it from the mother country the best traditions of the English bar, and, notwithstanding the shock of the Revolution, it has remained even to this day the most English of our institutions. The settlers of this country in the English colonies brought with them to America the English Common Law. During the later Colonial period, law was administered in accordance with the English procedure and according to English precedents. Many of the best-known lawyers, especially those in the southern colonies, received their legal training in the Inns of Court, in London. There in association with young lawyers, many of whom later became famous at the English bar, they acquired their knowledge of the English Common Law, profoundly influenced by those notions of right and personal liberty which characterized the legal thought of that period. From 1760, to the close of the Revolution, 115 Americans were admitted to the

Inns of Court; from South Carolina 47, from Virginia 21, from Maryland 16, from Pennsylvania 11, from New York 5, and from each of the other colonies one or two.

The influences which in England tended to give the bar an exclusive and aristocratic character operated even more strongly in the New World. The absence of any aristocracy based on hereditary privilege or military service, as well as the absence of a wealthy class and of the great fortunes won from industry and commerce, such as later characterized our economic development, gave to the legal profession an unquestioned ascendency in American social and political life.

One who reads with discrimination the history of the period of sixty years following the Revolution is impressed not only with the part played by lawyers in public affairs and in the development of law in this country, but with the fact that they played the part exceedingly well. The Constitution itself, legislation, notably for the establishment of the Federal and state governments, as well as the common law developed and formulated during that period, were not only on the whole the work of lawyers, but we may take a justifiable pride in the training, skill, and breadth of view with which that work was done.

The early history of the country is filled with the names of great lawyers, leaders in their profession, who not only wielded well a wide public influence, but made substantial and important contributions to the development of law in this country. John Marshall, the great Chief Justice of the United States, who more than any other one man made the Constitution of the United

States a vital, legal force; Chancellor Kent, whose Commentaries on American Law, originally written as lectures for delivery at Columbia College, have exerted as wide an influence on the development of the law in this country as any single book; Alexander Hamilton, William Pinkney, William Livingston, Rufus Choate, Daniel Webster, Story, Clay, Calhoun, Judge Shaw, Lincoln, Chase, and Judge Cooley, are a few of the many names which are significant of the position and influence of the bar during the formative period of our history.

During this period the corporate and professional tone of the American bar was high. A fortunate combination of influences worked together to stimulate both respect and zeal for high professional standards and to promote the fidelity, dignity, and standing of the profession. The great majority of lawyers lived and practised their profession in small communities. As late as 1840 the total number of lawyers in the whole country was about the same as or a little less than the membership of the bar in the city of Greater New York to-day. Until 1832 both Federal and state judges were appointed, usually by the executive with the consent and approval of the upper house of the legislative body, a practice which is continued down to the present time in the case of the Federal courts, but which has continued in a few only of the state courts. The bar exercised a powerful influence over the appointing power, and, following the English tradition, the judges were usually selected from among the leaders of the bar and appointed to office for long terms or during good behavior. Capable and experienced lawyers, known and indorsed by their professional associates, were thus invested with the great powers of the judicial office. The temptation of the judge to administer his office for political ends or to promote his own reëlection was thus removed at the outset by the method of his selection and by the judicial tenure. The judges knowing the members of the bar and being well known by them, and each being stimulated by the desire for the good opinion of the other, it was inevitable that each should react upon the other and that the result should be a zeal for professional skill and learning and an earnest desire and coöperative effort to promote the honor and dignity of the profession. Contributory influences undoubtedly were the homogeneity of race and the similarity of training and experience of the great majority of the lawyers. The social position and prestige of the bar, too, at a time when wealth had not yet become the measure of social standing that it has to-day, made its reputation for professional rectitude a possession to be cherished and defended.

It is difficult to overestimate the importance of sound training and correct professional standards of members of the bar to the administration of justice. The lawyer, upon his admission to the bar, becomes an official of the court, invested with extraordinary powers and privileges. In theory he is a minister of justice, and his highest duty is to aid and promote the administration of justice. For this purpose he is permitted to begin and terminate legislation in his client's name, to represent him in court, to determine upon and guide the course of litigation. The communications of his client made to him in a professional capacity are inviolable. He is a partisan and advocate only because experience has taught us, and our legal system has adopted the principle, that the controversial method is the best means of discovering the facts and the law which must control judicial decision. His partisanship, however, is limited always to a fair presentation of the facts and law which favor his client's case and subject always to his obligation to promote and not obstruct the cause of justice.

It is not my purpose to discourse on legal ethics or to attempt to formulate the essentially sound principles which underlie our system of legal ethics. But enough has been said of the larger duties and obligations of the lawyer to indicate at least that the proper administration of justice depends very largely, if not mainly, on the purpose, training, and morale of the members of the bar. Duties requiring as they do not only great learning but long and exacting experience, involving oftentimes a delicate perception of moral as well as legal obligation and a just appreciation of the claims of the state, can be performed properly only by a bar which has had thorough training and possesses the *esprit de corps* which results only from well-developed corporate feeling and professional pride. Pride in professional caste directed by precept and example of leaders of the bar and by the judges who are, or should be, themselves leaders of the bar, as it is in England and was in the early days of the Republic, is the most powerful single influence in aid of the proper administration of justice.

The early history of the bar in the United States is characterized by the close social and professional association of its members. The comparatively small number of the members of the bar and the custom of "riding circuit" undoubtedly stimulated this kind of activity. John Adams, in one of his letters, gives an attractive picture of the close personal relationship which existed among members of the Massachusetts bar in 1790. Speaking of the bar meetings, he said (letter to William Cranch, March 14, 1790):

"Many of these meetings were the most delightful entertainments I ever enjoyed. The spirit that reigned there was that of sense, generosity, honor, and integrity; and the consequence was most happy to the courts and the bar; instead scenes of wrangling, chicanery, quibbling, and ill manners were soon converted into order, decency, truth, and candor."

All the accounts of the activities of the profession which have come down to us from the letters, diaries and reminiscences of the first half of the nineteenth century, when the judges and lawyers rode circuit together, teem with references to the close association of lawyers and judges and its influence on the profession. As is said by Charles Warren in *A History of the American Bar*:

"Many older lawyers have been of the opinion that the largest and best part of legal education of the past was this mingling of the whole bar together in travelling together from county to county and from court to court, the enforced personal relations which were thus brought about and the presence of the younger members of the bar during the trials of cases by their seniors."

The impartial student of our legal system is compelled reluctantly to admit that, taking into account the entire history of the American bar, there has been a deterioration of our bar both in its personnel, its corporate morale, and, consequently, in the public influence wielded by it; and that this deterioration has been very considerably accelerated during the present generation. I do not base this conclusion upon the increasing number of disbarment proceedings which have blackened the annals of the bar in this county in recent years — indeed, this might be taken as an indication, rather, of a wholesome revival of professional spirit in this state.

My conclusion is based rather on the obvious loss of community interest and loss of pride of professional caste in the legal profession as a whole, and on the very general lack of friendly coöperation and of mutual interest and respect between the bar and the bench which characterized them in their early history. The reasons for this change are not far to seek, although they are fairly numerous and all worthy of some examination.

I have already referred to the fact that our bar inherited the best traditions of the English bar. Owing, however, to the spread of democratic ideas during and following the Revolution, some of the most characteristic features of the organization of the English bar were not copied here. Among these may be mentioned the method of calling candidates to the bar, the distinction between solicitors and barristers, and the method of selecting judges.

By the end of the reign of Edward I (1307) the King's Court, which in more primitive times had attended the king's person in his journeyings, had become permanently located at Westminster Hall in London, and was there attended by lawyers from all parts of the kingdom, who appear to have associated together with the same fraternity as later characterized the circuit riding bar of this country during the Colonial period and in the first half of the nineteenth century.

One of the consequences of this association was the gradual growth and organization of the voluntary associations of English lawyers known as the Inns of Court, which collectively might be likened in some respects to a university, organized for the study of law and preparation for admission to the bar. The exact origin of the Inns of Courts is lost in antiquity. The word "inn," derived from the French, originally signified the mansion of a person of rank or wealth. Inns of Court were originally believed to have been the inns or mansions leased by these societies of lawyers, which societies themselves, therefore, ultimately came to be known as the Inns of Court. The name came gradually to be applied to the four "Honorable Law Societies" of Lincoln's Inn, Gray's Inn, the Inner Temple, and the Middle Temple.

To the Inns of Court was delegated from the earliest time the regulation of admission to the English bar and the disciplining or disbarring of lawyers, powers which the four Inns of Court have retained to this day. Before one can become a candidate for admission to the English bar he must be admitted to an Inn and satisfy certain requirements of the Inn with respect to his legal study and training. His admission to the Inn, his examination for the bar, his final call to the bar, as well as measures for his discipline or disbarment throughout his professional career, are under the control of the "Benchers" or governing board of his Inn. The benchers of the several Inns have usually included in their numbers the most eminent members of the bench and bar. Thus the Benchers of the Inner Temple include, or included until very recently, in their numbers two ex-lord chancellors, five judges, and a speaker of the House of Commons, several peers of the realm, and other high officers and barristers of eminence.

The extent and thoroughness of legal education in the Inns of Court have been very variable in different periods of their history, but on its purely intellectual side it is undoubtedly much inferior to that now afforded by the better law schools in this country. The power and influence of the Inns of Court lies not so much in their purely educational activities as in the stimulation of professional ideals and the perpetuation of professional traditions, and in the almost unconscious exercise of a process of selection by which only the more fit reach the ultimate call to the bar. If we can imagine our own Bar Association having behind it the traditions of some six centuries as the guide and mentor of the legal profession, admitting to its membership students at the very beginning of their law study, and judging of their fitness for the profession after some years of close association with them, we can understand something of the part played by the English Inns of Court in maintaining the standards of the English bar.

A peculiarity of the English bar, due to the action of the Inns of Court taken about the middle of the sixteenth century, is the division of the lawyer class into barristers and attorneys or, as they are now called, solicitors. To the barrister was reserved the exclusive right of advocacy in court upon the retainer of a solicitor, the more routine part of practice, that is to say, the office practice, including the dealing with clients, the bringing of actions, the preparation or briefing of a case for trial by a barrister being exclusively within the province of the solicitor. Barristers alone were called to the bar by the Inns of Court, solicitors being admitted to practice by the court after serving a clerkship in a solicitor's office, and passing an examination, much as attorneys are admitted to the bar in the United States. The admission and disbarment of solicitors is now regulated in England by the Incorporated Law Society, an organization of solicitors incorporated under an act of Parliament. The distinction between the barristers, or counselors, as they were called in this country, and attorneys survived the Revolution for a time, notably in Massachusetts, New York, and New Jersey. The distinction was, however, dropped in all of the states in the early part of the nineteenth century, except in New Jersey, which still reserves to counselors alone the right to appear in its highest courts.

Undoubtedly the objection in America to the English classification of the members of the bar is that it creates a specially privileged class within a class already necessarily possessed of special power and privileges, and that it closes, or may close, the door of opportunity to the capable man. A pathetic consequence of the English system is the full-fledged barrister having within himself the capacity and possibilities of the great lawyer, yet unable to exhibit or develop them because of his inability to accept a retainer direct from the client. Professional business must come to him from the solicitor, whose patronage is too often dependent in the first instance upon personal or social influence. There is also a possible loss of efficiency in that the barrister does not personally consult with the client or witnesses, although this, I believe, is more than offset by the fact that he does not feel the personal pressure to extreme partisanship as does the American lawyer who consults his client and the witnesses as he tries his case. The barrister is thus able to assume a more detached and purely professional attitude toward his case than is the American trial lawyer.

The great advantage afforded by the English system from the public viewpoint is that it tends always to emphasize and perpetuate the professional spirit and high standards of professional conduct. It limits the number of those who are entitled to practise before its courts. It tends to confine its members to those who by character, training, and association are fit to bear its responsibilities. The result is that the skill, ease, and freedom from needless technicality and pettifogging with which English court proceedings are conducted is a revelation to an American lawyer.

It is noteworthy that in England cases of professional misconduct of barristers or cases requiring the disciplinary action of the Inns of Court are extremely rare, whereas cases of discipline of solicitors, who are admitted much as are attorneys in the United States, are comparatively frequent.

I believe that the good in the English system without the evil might have been preserved to us had the extreme democratic tendencies of the early nineteenth century permitted the state to claim and insist upon having the services exclusively of an aristocracy of character and training in the administration of its laws. This could have been accomplished either through the medium of an incorporated law society embracing the entire membership of the bar and controlling admission to it, as do the Inns of Court, or by the establishment of comprehensive and exacting preliminary training and examination for admission to the bar, leaving the young lawyer, however, free, after his admission to the bar, to accept his retainer directly from the client.

Following the American Revolution some effort was made to perpetuate the English tradition in this country in a number of states, notably in New York and Massachusetts. Voluntary associations of lawyers, known as Moots, Sodalities, or local bar associations, exerted very considerable influence on admission to the bar. By common consent then, and even during the Colonial period, a college education was regarded as essential to success at the bar. The lawyers at the Massachusetts bar between 1788 and 1817 were practically all college graduates. The majority were graduates of Harvard, with representatives from Dartmouth, Brown, and Williams. In 1805, 77 of the 105 members of the bar of New Hampshire were college graduates, and in Maine, Connecticut, New Jersey and South Carolina, a large proportion of the bar, and in New York, a somewhat smaller proportion, were either educated for the bar in England, or were graduates from American colleges, notably from Yale, Princeton, Kings, afterward Columbia College, the University of Pennsylvania, and William and Mary's College, of Virginia. This is in striking contrast to conditions which prevail to-day, when, notwithstanding our increased educational facilities, the men who complete a college education before applying for admission to the bar are in a small minority. In 1914, for example, only 40 per cent of the candidates for admission to the bar in New York were college graduates.

During the rapid development of Jeffersonian democracy in the first part of the nineteenth century there was a marked revulsion of feeling against the aristocratic pretensions of the bar, especially in the new western states. Admission to the bar came to be regarded not as a privilege to be extended by the state only to the more fit, but as a right to be availed of by all. The consequence of this reaction has been that for a considerable period in our history we have steadily lowered the standards of the bar, informal as they were, which prevailed during the Revolutionary period.

In many states little or no preliminary education is now required, and state examinations for admission to the bar when required are often farcical. When efforts have been made to make the tests more exacting, the result too often has been to make the examinations narrow and technical and to ignore altogether the broader questions of legal principle and legal history.

The democratic idea is carried to its extreme, for example, in Indiana, where by constitutional provision every voter is entitled as a matter of right to admission to the bar. Notwithstanding this ease of creating the class of "constitutional" lawyers, I am told that there are still many lawyers in Indiana who find it worth while to prepare themselves for the practice of their profession by a course of study at the best law schools in the country. Massachusetts has in the current year adopted a statute providing for preliminary education of candidates for admission to the bar substantially equivalent to a grammar school training.

New York has steadily raised the standards of admission to the bar and is now, on the whole, I believe, the most exacting of states in this respect. It is still possible, however, for a man to be admitted to the bar in New York who has never had the benefit of a high school education, although he must have studied law for four years before presenting himself for examination. The method of examination, too, leaves much to be desired. The questions are often narrowly technical in character and many subjects regarded by the best law schools as of great importance to the well-trained lawyer are not touched upon. The result of the methods of admission to the bar which have generally obtained throughout the United States is that they have set a low standard of character and attainment for the entire bar. In the hands of the incompetent or morally unsound man the license to practise law becomes a license to prey upon the weak and helpless; and in the hands of the well-disposed to whom is wanting the training and environment which develops character and intellectual capacity, it is a privilege destructive of the proper administration of justice.

An institution especially characteristic of the history of the legal profession in the United States is the professional law school. The first professorship of law in the United States was founded at Columbia, then Kings College, in 1773. James Kent, afterwards Chancellor Kent, was appointed to this professorship in 1794, and from his lectures given at Columbia after his retirement from the bench came his famous Commentaries. The first of the modern type of professional law schools was the famous Litchfield Law School. This was founded by Judge Tappan Reeve, at Litchfield, Connecticut, in 1784, and continued to receive law students until about 1833. The Harvard Law School was founded in 1817, and received its great impetus when Judge Story became a professor there in 1830. The Columbia Law School, under the leadership of Theodore Dwight, was reëstablished as a professional law school in 1858. Following the lead of these schools, there have now been established 116 professional law schools in the United States, maintaining professional law courses of from one to three years, and assuming to train their students for professional law practice.

The substitution of study in law schools for the old method of reading in a law office has had two quite different effects on the morale and intellectual qualifications of the American bar. Some of the schools have set standards much higher than those of the rules regulating admission to the bar, and have thus contributed their influence toward the movement for improved standards. In point of number, however, they have been outweighed by the schools which have allowed their standards to be set by the requirements for admission to the bar and which devote themselves merely to guiding their students by the easiest route to the bar. The lamentable result is that thousands of young men in the United States annually find their way to the bar, who are poorly qualified for its duties and responsibilities, and who, without the aid of the "cramming" law school, would have possessed neither the patience nor the force of character to have prepared themselves for their bar examinations.

To some extent all law schools are responsible for the waning of professional spirit and traditions. The lawyer of a generation ago received his training in the law office. There he gradually grew into his profession, absorbing unconsciously from his environment something of the professional ideals and traditions of the bar. Whatever may have been the faults of this method of training, and they are numerous and their number has increased under modern conditions, it was at least practical in character, and the young lawyer acquired by experience and from contact with the older lawyers something of the lawyer's point of view even before his admission to the bar. Under modern conditions, the candidate for admission to the bar spends three years or more in the law school, without any actual contact generally with the members of his profession. He may in most States be admitted to the bar and become a full-fledged lawyer without ever having spent as much as a day in a law office. It is therefore not strange that the present generation has witnessed a loss of the corporate spirit in the legal profession.

Another profound influence on the corporate spirit of our bar is the changing relation of the members of our bar to each other and to the judges. Increase in numbers, especially in the larger cities, accounts in part for a lack of community interest among members of the bar. Of the seventeen thousand lawyers in Greater New York, only about 35 per cent are members of any bar association. Any general acquaintance, to say nothing of coöperative effort, among its membership is obviously impossible.

The change of relationship between the bar and the bench is due to increase of the members of the bar, but even more to the changed methods of selecting judges. Following the generally adopted change from the appointive to the elective system the judges, especially in the lower courts, have very generally been selected because of their political service or availability. Professional standing and the indorsement of the bar have been too often secondary considerations in their selection, indeed if they have received any consideration at all.

The professional influence and leadership which our judges formerly exercised, and which to-day are so characteristic of the English judicial system, have thus been seriously impaired in the United States, and this is undoubtedly one of the contributing causes of the deterioration of the bar.

The tremendous economic changes which took place in this country during the last century have also exercised a powerful influence on the bar. The establishment and growth of the railroads, the development of vast industrial corporations, have not only expanded enormously both the statute and the common law, but they have given us a new type of lawyer and a new leadership at the bar. For the leadership of the advocate and the legal scholar the march of economic development has tended to substitute the leadership of the business lawyer, who at his best is the skillful, resourceful solicitor, a specialist in corporation law, and who, at his worst, is the mere hired man of corporations.

Such leadership, at its best, while none the less honorable, has tended, nevertheless, to give to the practice of law the characteristics of business rather than that of a learned profession, and has contributed its part toward destroying the corporate spirit and activity which characterized the profession during the earlier period.

It is hardly necessary to comment on the importance to the law and its administration of a bar of high character and efficiency. Present tendencies are fraught with danger to our institutions unless they are effectively checked. The ends to be attained are more exacting requirements for admission to the bar which conform to sound educational standards, and the stimulation and preservation in every possible way of the professional spirit and corporate feeling of the bar. Character may be inquired into and tested to some extent by character examinations. Continued association of the candidate with members of the bar whose own organization possesses exclusive authority to call the candidate to the bar, as do the Inns of Court, would, however, be much more effective. Examination as to training and intellectual fitness when committed to the courts has invariably been loosely administered, due, doubtless, to the pressure of immediate, but certainly not more important, judicial duties. It is believed that an improvement would be worked either by committing the whole subject to the charge of the state bar associations or state departments of education, or to a state commission appointed by the governor, the choice depending on local conditions. The signs are not wanting of a revival of interest in this subject and that serious attention will, in the not distant future, be more generally given to it. The campaign initiated by the New York City Bar Association against recreant attorneys, under the direction and sympathetic coöperation of Appellate Division of the Supreme Court, resulting in many disbarments, the searching examination into the character of candidates for admission to the bar in this judicial department, the adoption of codes of professional ethics by the American and various state bar associations, and the discussion of methods of examining for the bar at meetings of the American Bar Association, all indicate an aroused and growing public and professional interest in the subject, which will be, it is earnestly hoped, productive of improved conditions.

Discussion of this phase of the subject should not be closed without a word of qualification. While I have dwelt at some length on the deterioration of the bar which has taken place during the past generation, it is a deterioration which has resulted mainly from the lowering of the average by the influx to the bar of greater numbers of the unfit. Examples are not wanting of lawyers conspicuously fitted, by character and attainment, for the practice of their profession, and there is now at the bar, as there always has been and always will be, a considerable body of men who individually and collectively exhibit qualifications of character, learning, and skill worthy of the best traditions of the American Bar. The great problem for us as citizens is to make their influence greater and more respected, both in and out of the profession.

The judiciary of our country falls naturally into two

great classes, the Federal and the state. The Federal judiciary is made up of the nine judges of the Supreme Court, the district judges who, under recent amendment of the Judiciary Act, exercise original jurisdiction in law, equity, admiralty, bankruptcy, and in criminal and other cases arising under the Constitution and laws of the United States, and the circuit judges who, under the Judiciary Act, exercise appellate jurisdiction on appeals from the District Courts. They also hear in the first instance certain actions, notably proceedings brought by the government for violations of statutes relating to interstate commerce. There are 101 district and 30 circuit judges. All are appointed by the President, with the advice and consent of the Senate. They are appointed for life, and by Federal statute they are permitted to retire with a pension on reaching the age of seventy years. They may be removed from office only for high crimes and misdemeanors, by impeachment by the House of Representatives before the Senate.

There is a general similarity in the organization of the judiciary of the several states. The state courts consist, usually, of a court having original jurisdiction in law and equity and in criminal cases, holding their sessions at the various county seats, and known variously as circuit courts, superior courts, and in New York as the Supreme Court. From these courts appeals lie to a court having appellate jurisdiction only, and variously known as the Supreme Court, or Court of Appeals. In some states, of which Illinois and New York are typical, there are intermediate appellate courts sitting in the different judicial districts of the state. In New York our highest appellate court is the Court of Appeals, consisting of seven judges. There are four Appellate Divisions of the Supreme Court, having an intermediate appellate jurisdiction. Judges of the Appellate Division are designated by the governor from the judges of the Supreme Court, each court sitting in one of the four judicial departments of the state.

Most of the state judges sit both as law and equity judges. New Jersey, however, still maintains a separate equity system, presided over by a Chancellor and aided by the Vice-Chancellors who sit in various parts of the state to hear equity cases exclusively. In all of the states there are separate courts exercising their jurisdiction over the settlement of decedents' estates, the appointment and settlement of the accounts of executors, administrators, testamentary trustees, guardians, etc., known as surrogates' courts, probate courts, or orphans' courts. Their jurisdiction is statutory, but they possess substantially the jurisdiction of the ancient Ecclesiastical Courts of England, with some additions. In many states there are inferior courts for the trial of criminal cases, like our own courts of General and Special Sessions; and there are everywhere magistrates' courts for the trial of petty criminal cases, and with jurisdiction to hold prisoners for the action of the grand jury. There are also generally courts of inferior jurisdiction, having authority to try petty civil cases. Mention should also be made of the children's and domestic relations' courts, of comparatively recent origin in some of our large cities, the former having authority to try petty criminal offenses of children, and the latter both criminal and civil cases arising out of the relation of husband and wife and parent and child. Such is substantially the organization of the courts throughout the United States.

There is, perhaps, no function of government which touches more vitally the interests of the whole people or affects more permanently their well-being than the administration of justice through the courts. Under our system of law its successful administration must depend primarily upon the character, training, and skill of the judges, although, as I have already pointed out, it is materially affected by the character and training of the bar, and it is correspondingly difficult to have a bench of high character unless its labors are aided by a bar of high character, which exercises a potent influence in the selection of judges.

The English tendency has always been to magnify the power and influence of the judge. There is in England no popular dissatisfaction with the judges or their administration of justice, and a critical observer finds much to commend and little to criticize in English judicial history, certainly for the past 200 years or more. James Bryce, an extremely competent and accurate observer of American affairs, makes an interesting comparison of English and American judges in his *American Commonwealth.* He says:

"For some centuries Englishmen have associated the idea of power, dignity, and intellectual eminence with the judicial office, and tradition shorter, no doubt, but of respectable length, has made them regard it as incorruptible. The judges are among the greatest permanent officials of the state. They have earned their place by success more or less brilliant, but almost always considerable, in the struggles of the bar. They are removable by the crown only on the address of both houses of parliament. They enjoy large incomes and great social respect. Some of them sit in the House of Lords; some are members of the Privy Council. . . . The criticisms of an outspoken press rarely assail their ability; hardly ever their fairness. Even the bar which watches them daily, which knows all their ins and outs both before and after their elevation, treats them with more respect than is commonly shown by the clergy to the bishops."

After commenting on the fact that the Federal judiciary, notwithstanding the small salaries of the judges, has very generally been composed of men of ability and experience, who command general respect, he speaks of the state judges as follows:

"In six or seven commonwealths, of which Massachusetts is the best example among the eastern, and Michigan among the western states, they stand high; that is to say, the bench will attract the prosperous barrister, although he will lose in income, or the law professor, though he may lose his leisure; but in some states it is otherwise. A place on the bench of the supreme court carries with it little honor and commands slight social consideration. It raises no presumption that its holder is able or cultivated or trusted by his fellow-citizens. . . . Often he stands below the leader of the state or city bar in all these points."

He enumerates the causes which have lowered the quality of the state judges as follows: the smallness of the salaries paid, the limited terms of office, and the method of appointment, nominally by popular election, actually by the agency of party wire-pullers.

Upon the adoption of the Federal Constitution and the organization of the various state governments, the English system of appointment of judges for life or during good behavior was completely accepted and incorporated into our law. The selection of United States Supreme Court judges was made appointive by the Constitution. The Judiciary Act adopted by Congress in 1789 adopted the same policy with respect to the selection of all the inferior Federal judges, and such has continued to be our policy with respect to the Federal judges down to the present day. The same policy was adopted by each of the original states and continued to be the policy of all the states, with the exception of Georgia, until 1832. In 1812 the state of Georgia adopted the policy of electing certain inferior court judges. In 1832 the state of Mississippi adopted a constitution which provided for the popular election of all judges who were to be elected to the judicial office for short terms. The example of Mississippi was followed by the majority of states, so that to-day popular election is the established method of selecting judges in all the states of the union, except in Connecticut, Delaware, Maine, New Jersey, New Hampshire, Massachusetts, Rhode Island, South Carolina, Vermont, and Virginia. In Connecticut, Delaware, Massachusetts, and New Jersey, judges are appointed during good behavior by the governor with the consent of the Senate or the Council. In Rhode Island, South Carolina, Vermont, and Virginia, the judges are appointed by the Legislature for short terms of office. The elective system was adopted in New York by the Constitution of 1846.

There is no record of the debates of the Constitutional Convention, which adopted the Mississippi Constitution of 1832. Judging, however, from the proceedings of the later Constitutional Conventions which adopted the elective system, the change in the method of selecting judges is not attributable to the desire to remedy any recognized abuses, but rather to the spread of democratic ideas during the first of the last century, which ultimately resulted in making practically all state officers elective, and which has brought about in our own day the reaction in favor of the short ballot.

It would, in fact, be difficult to discover any specific evil which it was hoped or believed would be prevented by a change from the appointive to the elective system. We must look, rather, to the reaction led by Jefferson against representative government as developed by the Federalist party and to the popular belief in the political philosophy which accepts without reservation the doctrine that every function of government, however much special knowledge, training, and skill is required for its performance, can be best exercised by the people through the ballot. If it is true that the judge should possess professional skill and training and some influence with the bar over which he is to preside, his selection should be made by a responsible officer of the government who has authority and opportunity to make special investigation, and who can weigh the evidence as to the merits of the respective candidates quite as much as in the selection of officers for military or naval service, or government engineers, chemists, or health officers.

There can be little doubt that the substitution of the elective for the appointive system has, on the whole, had an evil effect upon both the American bench and bar. Too often its practical operation has been to substitute for the choice of the responsible executive the choice of the irresponsible political boss or wire-puller. The judge would be more than human if he did not recognize the influences which had brought about his election, and in those states where the election is for short terms, the desire for reëlection must invariably exert its influence on the judicial conduct. Above all, he knows that he owes correspondingly little to the bar, and that his power for leadership in his own profession is of little value in the struggle for election to judicial office. The whole tendency is to substitute political availability for proved probity and skill as a test of qualification for judicial office.

Efforts of the bar to influence judicial selection or to bring about judicial nomination independent of political considerations have very generally proved abortive. The people have always shown a lively concern in and great sensitiveness as to the selection of judges whenever the candidates have been charged with specific acts of misconduct, and the office to be filled is a high one. But almost invariably, in the case of the lower courts, or where the question at issue was one of general fitness and professional standing and of the political influences back of the candidate, the people have shown themselves apathetic.

A comparison of the Federal bench with that of the states where the elective system prevails, as was noted by Mr. Bryce, leads to the conclusion that, on the whole, the effect of the change has been unfortunate and that a return to the old system is one of the first and most important steps towards improvement in law administration in the United States, and this conclusion seems not any the less valid when one takes into account the excellent bench in states like Massachusetts and New Jersey, which have retained the appointive system; and it is worthy of note that in those states there is little evidence of dissatisfaction with the administration of law.

It is indeed remarkable that with a system so fraught with possibilities of public injury we have escaped to so great a degree actual corruption and public scandal. It is true that judges in New York, as an aftermath of the Tweed Ring exposures, were impeached and removed from office for corrupt practices; but the charge to be laid at the door of our elective system of choosing judges is rather that it has resulted in a lowering in tone and professional character of both bench and bar, and has deprived the bench of that leadership and public confidence to which it should be legitimately entitled. In New York the Court of Appeals, its highest court, through a long and honorable history, has preserved a high reputation for capacity and integrity. Notwithstanding some severe criticisms of a political character, which, it seems to the dispassionate observer, had no substantial foundation either in law or in ethics, it is believed that this court still possesses and deserves the confidence of the people. The four Appellate Divisions, since their creation under the Constitution of 1894, have established a high reputation for probity and ability, a fact which is due in part, at least, to the constitutional provision that the judges designated to sit in these courts should be selected by the executive.

Some of the unfortunate tendencies of the elective system apparent in other states have been mitigated in New York by our policy of electing judges for long terms. Fourteen years is the constitutional term of office of both Supreme Court and Court of Appeals judges. Nevertheless, there have been many examples of election of judges who would probably never have reached that office under an appointive system, and whose judicial careers have had anything but a beneficial effect on the administration of justice in this state. There have been some regrettable cases where just judges of proved capacity for judicial labors have failed of reëlection because of the exigencies of politics or because they were not sufficiently subservient to political interests; and for more than a generation we have been compelled to take note of the steadily widening gap between the bar and the judges, in whose selection the bar has so small a part.

The recall of judges apparently has lost vitality as a political issue in this country, and only passing reference need now be made to it. The fundamental objection to it is that it renders the judiciary still more subservient to political influences, when every teaching of history and experience is that these influences ought to be diminished. And it subjects judges to removal, and perhaps disgrace, without any organized or deliberative inquiry, and without opportunity to them to be heard before any body exercising judicial or quasi-judicial powers.

On the other hand, our experience has been that the removal by impeachment is a cumbersome and unwieldy proceeding, so difficult of application that it is likely to be invoked only in the most flagrant cases of judicial misconduct. The method of removal based on the English practice, in force in Massachusetts and New Jersey, where the judges may be removed by the Governor on the joint address of the two houses of the Legislature, seems to possess most of the safeguards of removal by impeachment, without its disadvantages.

The faithful and efficient performance of judicial duties is a subject possessing few attractions for the latter-day newspaper man and the writer of muck-raking magazine articles. Amid the swelling volume of criticism of judges and their administration of the law, and influenced by our desire for commendable reforms, we are prone to overlook altogether the fidelity and capacity with which, under our existing system, so many judges throughout the length and breadth of our land are performing the duties of the judicial office.

The decision in the Ives case, which called down on the judges who decided it such a storm of criticism, was rendered in the year 1911. The volumes containing the decisions of the Court of Appeals during that year contain the record of 749 decisions. Of these 749 decisions, only the Ives case seems to have been the subject of any serious criticism. The whole record of the proceedings of the court for the year 1911, regardless of the view we may take of the Ives case, is therefore one of remarkable diligence, capacity, and efficiency, of which the general public have very little knowledge or appreciation.

At a recent gathering of lawyers assembled in this city to honor the presiding judge of the Appellate Division in this department for his long years of service on the bench, one of the speakers, a member of his own court, truthfully said of him:

"During the seventeen years in which Judge Ingraham has acted as judge he has participated in the decision of 15,295 calendar cases and has written 2553 opinions. He takes all the motions made before the court, and last year there were 754. He reads all the records in disciplinary proceedings, constantly consulting with the Committee on Character, and surveying its work. He is kept in close touch with the work of the two Bar Associations. He makes, alters, revises, and enforces the rules, and deals with a great number of other important matters. His ability to dispatch business is almost phenomenal, and the record of the Appellate Division in this respect is extraordinary. After the first three months of the term the calendar is cleared each month.

"He minimizes technicalities, uses every effort to simplify and hasten procedure, regards a lawyer who betrays his client or deceives the court as a traitor to his profession and an enemy to the state. 'His soul flames with righteous indignation.' He has driven his associates with a velvet gloved, but no less steel-knuckled hand, up to his own standard of incessant work. To do that work he has contributed the highest intellectual qualities: knowledge of the law, fertility of resource, wide acquaintance with New York, broad sympathy, common sense, and a passionate desire for justice."

I refer to this occurrence, not because I regard the career of this judge as particularly unique, except in the point of years of service, but because his life work is typical of the service which is being rendered by many judges throughout the length and breadth of the land. Under any system of selection of judges there have always been such judges, and let us hope always will be. To such judges is due the orderly growth of law and its wise and just administration throughout the Anglo-Saxon world. One of the most important duties of citizenship is the unremitting effort to select such judges for the bench, and to maintain them in judicial position, and to honor them for arduous service well performed.

VIII

LAW REFORM

REGARDLESS of his prejudices one could not fail to be impressed with the widespread and persistent criticism of the administration of law in this country. Newspapers, popular magazines, political speeches, the utterances of social reformers, and not infrequently the graver pronouncements of more responsible critics, abound with disparaging references, not to say direct attacks, upon the courts and the legal profession. In weighing and assigning a proper value to these manifestations, some account may well be taken of the fact that the strident voice of protest and discontent not infrequently rises above the chorus of the satisfied, and that the weight of one's sorrows is often not measured by the volume of his lamentations.

Certainly, as has been pointed out in an earlier chapter, the volleys of criticism which have been directed toward the Ives case as decided by the Court of Appeals was entirely disproportionate to any practical inconvenience which flowed from that decision, and they left quite out of account the vast volume of judicial business regularly and satisfactorily disposed of by that court. Similar observation might be made of most of the cases which have given rise to the adverse criticism of courts.

One must also make some allowance for the vagaries of a period, now, happily, drawing to a close, I believe, more characterized by fantastic political theories and by vague and impractical aspirations for sudden social reform than have characterized any previous period in our political history. Nevertheless, when such allowances are made, disinterested and competent observers, as President Eliot, for example, come to the conclusion that a very considerable portion of the people believe that law is administered with too great regard for technicality and with too little regard for substantial justice, and that litigants are subjected to needless burdens and delays in securing their rights, and that such belief on the part of the people is not without some justification.

One is compelled to note, too, the disturbing frequency of trials resulting in determinations which are shocking to one's sense of propriety and justice. Without singling out cases for invidious comparison, one may call to mind cases decided in our own state in the last few years, where defendants charged with and undeniably guilty of serious crimes were acquitted by juries, or if convicted, were sentenced to grossly inadequate punishment. Such cases, taken quite at random, are fairly typical of a considerable number of others decided in various states of the country, an examination of which leaves one with the uncomfortable conviction that in them justice has failed, that all our precautions have been in vain, and that our elaborate machinery for the administration of law has broken down.

Our conclusion would hardly be just or trustworthy, however, if we failed to recognize that cases like these constitute a small minority among the thousands of cases which proceed to a just result without attracting public attention or comment. Nevertheless, we should cease to progress if we did not inquire into the causes of failures of justice and seek a remedy for defects in our judicial system, at least so far as failures of justice are attributable to such defects. At the outset, however, it will be necessary to indicate some of the limitations which, by the very nature of law and the necessities of its administration, are imposed on any program of law reform. And then as we see more clearly the possible and practicable, we may perhaps avoid the impracticable and the impossible.

That water cannot rise above its source is a law recognized clearly enough in natural science; but the like principle applied to theories of social organization is too often disregarded by some of our social and legal philosophers. Law has its source in the desire of civilized communities for justice, and in the belief that justice can be attained only through the adoption and application of a system of law; but law, as a medium of justice, can never rise above its source. If public sentiment is essentially lawless, if it is swayed by passion or prejudice, if, controlled by such influences, it demands that rules of law, however wise and salutary in principle, be disregarded in special cases, it is inevitable that juries should be foresworn and that judges should be found to distort the law.

The great fact to be reckoned with in the history of the English Common Law is that underlying and supporting it there has always been a popular love of justice and the belief that the kind of justice which would best serve the social welfare is justice according to law. It is this fact which has made the English Common Law the great force which it has been in western civilization. It is this sentiment which makes the weak and faithless juryman feel the weight of an outraged public sense of justice, and makes the unsuccessful litigant bow to the decision of the court without, at least publicly, reviling it. Without public faith and belief in justice according to law, any system of law, however skilfully devised, is but an empty form.

It is beyond the scope of this chapter to make any extensive investigation or comparison for the purpose of ascertaining whether there is a waning of the popular desire for justice according to law in this country. Statistics show, I believe, that there is a decrease in the number of lynchings and cases of mob law, which have been the disgrace and still disgrace the administration of justice in this country. On the other hand, the evidence is not wanting that juries are too often swayed by prejudice or by maudlin sentimentality, to disregard laws, the soundness and morality of which are not open to question.

The popular criticism of law and courts, now, happily, somewhat subsiding, has exhibited an intemperateness and lack of sense of propriety which can be wholly accounted for only by lack of popular faith in legal justice and by a willingness to substitute for it the notions of social and political quacks. Without attempting to measure the extent of this change in popular sentiment, or to judge as to its permanency, it will be sufficient if we keep steadily in mind that no amount of law reform will ever give legal justice to a people who themselves are indifferent to it or who are controlled by passion or prejudice, or class selfishness, rather than by the love of and faith in justice administered according to some settled principles of law.

Another fact fundamental in any scheme of law reform is so obvious that, like many others of the more obvious facts of life, we are prone to overlook its true significance. Law must necessarily be administered by human agencies. Assuming a perfect system for the administration of justice, unless the human agents who administer the system are likewise perfect, a perfect result cannot be hoped for. When the other great operations of the civilized world are carried forward without loss, friction, or blunder, it will be time to demand perfection in the human agencies which make and administer our laws.

At the very foundation, therefore, of any just and adequate legal system must lie the popular desire for justice, the firm belief in justice according to law, possessing the characteristics of generality and certainty. United with this must exist a deep public concern in the selection of fit agencies for law administration, the judges and lawyers, resulting in methods of selection best adapted to that end. If these qualities in the public temper are wanting, our discussion of remedies for failures of justice, of the law's delays, its technicalities, its lack of recognition of social needs, is a discussion of symptoms only, and not the disease. The true law reform, therefore, begins with the stimulation in the public mind of the love of justice, its education as to the nature of law, and the grave importance of delegating its administration only to those who are fit to bear that responsibility.

Judges and lawyers not only administer law; they

make the common law and they give to much of the written law its character and effectiveness. The character of the judges and lawyers of this generation will determine the character of the law of the next.

If every citizen, or even a majority of our citizens, recognized the true significance of this statement, is it credible that for any length of time we would continue, as in the majority of the United States, to admit men to the bar with the barest smattering of legal training and general education and select our judges on the basis of political expediency or, as is too often the case, at the dictation of the political boss? In the last chapter I pointed out at some length the pernicious effect of our neglect of matters so vital to the standing and efficiency of the legal profession. I refer to them now only for the purpose of again calling your attention to the fact that they have a direct and immediate effect on those phases of law administration which are so much the subject of popular criticism. Of what avail to complain of the law's delays when thousands of men are admitted to the bar whose professional ideals admit of their bringing groundless actions or interposing groundless defenses?

Of what avail to seek some formal cure for the law's technicalities when we examine candidates for the bar mainly with respect to their knowledge of technicalities and send them to the bar imbued with the notion that the license to practise law is a privilege to play a game in technicalities at the expense of their clients? What boots it to complain of the law's delays and advocate special measures for the prevention of the law's delays, when the time of the court may be wasted by lawyers not competent or prepared to try their cases or who force the court to read volumes of affidavits loaded down with trivial and irrelevant matter, because it dares not accept at face value the statement of counsel made in open court.

In England there is very little criticism of the legal system and no serious problem of law reform. I think I understood the reason for this after I had spent a morning at one of the law courts in London last summer. The court was what was known as the Vacation Court; not a court for the trial of cases, but for the hearing of special motions requiring attention during the summer vacation. The court was presided over by a judge distinguished, as are most of the English judges, for his learning and ability, elevated to the bench by appointment to his office for life. The court-room was thronged with barristers called to the bar through the medium of the Inns of Courts, which were described in the last lecture. As the barristers arose in turn to present their cases to the court, each did so with a simplicity and directness indicative of a reserve power founded on thorough training and experience. His opponent replied in like manner. A few well-directed questions from the bench, and the exact question of law or fact stood revealed, stripped of all extraneous matter. The court's decision was promptly given from the bench, the case was then disposed of, and the next case was called. There was no unseemly wrangling, no waste of time of the court. The questions of the presiding judge were answered frankly, without reservation, and it was obvious that the court in rendering its decision could and did rely on the statements of counsel made in the course of the argument.

Contrast this practice with the scenes which regularly take place in our own similar court for the hearing of contested motions. After a day of listening to prolonged argument, more or less relevant to the motions pending before him, the judge reserves his decision, retires to his chamber, where he devotes his attention for days, perhaps weeks or months, to reading and sifting voluminous affidavits submitted to him, in order that he may ascertain what the motions which he has already heard are really about, and what their merits really are.

The ease and facility with which the English court disposed of its judicial business depended in part upon the fact that the English procedure is simpler than our own, but mainly upon the fact that the judge possessed preëminent professional qualifications for his office, and that the barristers in his court were a selected group fitted by training and character to participate in the administration of justice.

With lawyers capable of presenting their cases in court and with too high a regard for their professional position to distort the law or the facts, and with judges capable of grasping the real issues of law and fact involved, possessing the power to control the course of judicial business pending before them, and the will to exercise it, the problem of the law's delays and its technicalities is reduced to a minimum. Improvement of bench and bar, the removal of the bench, so far as possible, from political influences, and the restoration to the judges in many of our states of the power which should properly be exercised by them, lie at the root of the problem of law reform. Without these, one may devote himself in vain to what may be called the subsidiary problems of law reform, that is to say, the mere formal legislative changes which affect in a more or less perfunctory manner those features of law administration, which are now so much the subject of popular discussion.

Let us now, however, turn to what I have termed some of the subsidiary problems of law reform. Among the criticisms of our legal system are the charges that our procedure is too complicated and technical, that there are too many appeals, that there are needless delays and technical difficulties in the selection of juries in cases which excite general public interest, that the proof of facts involving scientific questions by expert witnesses has been subject to grave abuses, that the law is dilatory, the trial and final disposition of causes often being excessively delayed, that the administration of justice, which ought to be simple, direct, and easily accomplished, is, in fact, complicated and burdensome.

It will be observed that all of these criticisms, except those relating to the law's delays, are directly involved in our system of procedure. Whatever will improve our system of procedure will improve conditions with respect to each of these criticisms. For nearly fifty years our system of procedure has been under the direct control of the legislature, and, as was pointed out in the lecture on that subject, the volume of our procedural law, its complexity, and its technicality, have steadily increased. In the discussion of this subject, a possible method of improvement was suggested by delegating the power and duty of enacting rules of procedure to the judges exclusively. But whatever the method adopted, any plan whereby the number of formal provisions governing procedure is reduced, the power and discretion of the court in procedural matters increased, and the power for frequent and haphazard amendment limited, will ultimately result in some simplification of our procedure and in lessening the cause for just dissatisfaction with our procedural law.

From time immemorial, the "law's delays" has been the subject of the bitter jibe of the layman. On my desk lies a copy of *De Laudibus Legum Angliæ,* written before the discovery of America, by Sir John Fortesque, who was Chief Justice of England, and afterward Lord Chancellor to King Henry VI. In the dialogue supposed to occur between the Lord Chancellor and the young prince, whom he is instructing as to the excellences of the English common law, the prince is made to say:

> "There remains but one thing, my Chancellor, to be cleared up, which makes me hesitate, and gives me disgust. If you can satisfy my doubts in this particular, I will cease to importune you with any more queries. It is objected that the laws of England admit of great delays in the course of their proceedings beyond what the laws in other countries allow of. This is not only a distraction to justice, but often an insupportable expense to the parties who are at law, especially in such actions where the demandant is not entitled to his damages";

to which the Lord Chancellor replied in effect, after pointing out that the delays were not greater in England than in France,

> "But it is really necessary that there should be delays in legal proceedings, provided they are not too dilatory and tedious. . . . Judge-

ment is never so safe when the process is hurried. I remember once at an Assises, a jail delivery at Saulsbury, that I saw a woman indicted for the death of her husband within the year. She was found guilty and burned for the same. . . . At a subsequent Assises I saw a servant of the man who was so killed, tried and convicted before the same judge for the same murder. He made ample confession that he was the only person who was guilty of the said fact."

This passage from Sir John is interesting, first, because it informs us that the complaint as to the law's delays is by no means a new one, and because it reminds us that some delay in the law's procedure is not an unmixed evil.

Many critics of the law's delays speak as though the judicial protection of one's rights was to be obtained with the same ease with which one orders a suit of clothes from his tailor, and that justice is a commodity to be freely obtained without trouble or annoyance.

If, however, one conceives that his rights have been impaired and that the matter is of sufficient importance to induce him to resort to the courts, he naturally desires his case to be carefully prepared and skilfully presented. Preparation of the case involves a study of the facts and of the law by his lawyer, the collection of evidence, the examination of witnesses, often the investigation of accounts, the examination of documents and of papers, the drawing of pleadings, — involving prolonged study and investigation and requiring like professional service on the part of the attorney for the defendant. These tasks require time, and in performing them we have no more right to expect the work of the lawyer to be hastily and imperfectly done than we have to expect like neglect when important problems are submitted for solution to the engineer, the architect, or the scientist.

A not unimportant consequence of reasonable deliberation in proceeding with the trial of cases is that opportunity is thus afforded for the litigants to settle their disputes without actually proceeding to a trial. Time tends to soften the anger and correct the mistakes and errors of judgment, which are the fruitful causes of legal controversy. It is, therefore, not a fault, but a virtue, in judicial procedure that it proceeds without haste, with full opportunity for deliberation on the part of the litigants and for preparation on the part of counsel, so that the result may ultimately put an end to controversy and leave us satisfied that justice has been done.

Nevertheless, when the trials of cases are postponed two or more years, as has been the case in this and many other states, until witnesses and counsel have forgotten what the case was about and witnesses have perhaps died or disappeared, and meanwhile the plaintiff, if his case is just, has been denied his rights; or, again, when the case has been tried and appealed and a new trial ordered perhaps two or three or even more times, we have just reason to complain of the law's delays and make some inquiry as to the cause. There are many special causes operating to make delays in judicial procedure one of the crying evils of our legal system, and almost without exception they have their origin either in the failure of the members of the bar to live up to proper professional standards, or in the faults of our system of procedure, to which reference was made in the chapter on that subject. If, for example, every case needlessly begun or needlessly defended because of the incompetence of the counsel or because of the willingness of counsel to stir up unnecessary litigation could be stricken from the court calendars, I venture to say there would be no serious problem of delay in reaching cases for trial after they had been placed upon the calendar.

"Discourage litigation," said Abraham Lincoln to the young lawyer. "Persuade your neighbors to compromise whenever you can. Point out to them how the nominal winner is often the real loser in fees, expenses, and waste of time. As a peacemaker the lawyer has a superior opportunity to be a good man. Never stir up litigation. A worse man can scarcely be found than one who does this. Who can be more nearly a fiend than he who habitually overhauls the registry of deeds in search of defects in title, whereupon to stir up strife and put money into his pocket." Lincoln not only stated the duty of the lawyer, recognized by our code of ethics, but he touched upon one of the prime causes of the crowding of our court calendars and of the law's delay. I think the better class of lawyers recognize the morality as well as the practical good sense of Lincoln's advice.

A great volume of litigation for which neither lawyers nor our methods of procedure are wholly responsible is due to the vast increase in accident litigation for which there is common-law liability, especially in cities and industrial centers. The volume of this litigation greatly exceeds that of all other classes of litigation combined. Its wastefulness and its essential injustice under modern industrial conditions have been fully revealed in the public discussion which has led to the enactment of the various workmen's compensation acts, and these, where successfully established, should enormously reduce the number of litigated claims arising out of injuries to the employees, for the reason that the statute imposes liability on the employer without his fault and does away with the defenses of assumption of risk, contributory negligence, and the fellow-servant rule, which have been so fruitful of litigation.

The possibility of making a similar reduction in the amount of litigation growing out of the injuries to persons other than employees which are incident to the business of public service companies is a problem worthy of consideration. At present, the court calendars the country over are clogged with cases of this class. The larger corporations have generally adopted the policy of settling just accident claims when they can be settled on a fair basis, so that a considerable proportion of the litigated cases are brought in the hope of gaining some unmerited advantage by playing on the sympathies and prejudices of a jury. This method of enforcing liability is wasteful in the extreme. The cases are often taken on the contingent-fee basis, and the proceeds go mainly to benefit the ambulance-chasing attorney, and not the victim of the injury.

A serious cause of the law's delay, as well as a prolific source of professional misconduct and scandal, would be summarily removed if, as suggested by Moorfield Storey in his book on "Law Reform," the losses arising from injuries incident to the business of public carriers could be distributed by the medium of a compulsory insurance scheme, the cost of which should be borne by the carrier, but taken into account in fixing its rates. This, of course, at its best, is a poor substitute for the evils which are mainly attributable to the unworthy members of the bar and to an unfortunate system of procedure. But it would, I believe, be infinitely preferable to the conditions which now exist.

The delays which take place after a case has been placed on the calendar and is ready for trial are due for the most part to the peculiarities of procedure, the excessive time and attention devoted to the selection of a jury, the double appeal, the reluctance or statutory inability of appellate courts in some states when error has been committed to correct the error in a proper case by modifying the judgment or reversing it, and entering a final judgment, instead of sending the case back for a new trial one, two, or even more times. These are causes of delay which are capable of remedy. The number of peremptory challenges to jurymen as fixed by statute might be reduced. The absurd practice in many states, under which a man who has sufficient intelligence to have formed an opinion about a case of general public knowledge and interest may be disqualified to serve as a juryman, should be abolished, and, above all, we would expedite the business of courts and give litigants and juries the benefit of the learning and experience of our judges and increase their power over the conduct of litigation.

In several states judges are denied the power to limit the time of argument of counsel or to compel counsel to limit the scope of their arguments to the evidence. Notwithstanding the fact that our judges are given the exclusive power to try questions of fact in equity cases, and that their experience in trials would be of great practical assistance to a jury, they are, in a majority of states, prohibited from expressing any opinion on the evidence to the jury, and in some states it is dangerous for them even to comment on the evidence. Instead of laying a firm hand on the proceedings of a trial, as do the English judges, and our Federal judges, and guiding the trial for the purpose of securing a just result, our state judges in many states are practically limited to acting as a presiding officer, without substantial power, except to rule on the evidence. As was said by Mr. Justice Brewer (Patton *vs.* Railroad Company, 179 U. S., 660):

"The judge is primarily responsible for the just outcome of the trial. He is not a mere moderator of a town meeting, submitting questions to the jury for determination, nor simply ruling on the admissibility of testimony, but one who, in our jurisprudence, stands charged with full responsibilities."

As was said by Mr. Justice Gray, of the U. S. Supreme Court:

"Trial by jury in the courts of the United States is a trial presided over by a judge with authority not only to rule upon objections to evidence and to instruct the jury upon the law, but also when, in his judgement, the due administration of justice requires it to aid the jury by explaining and commenting upon and even giving them his opinion upon questions of fact, provided only he submits those questions to their determination."

The power of the judge to set a verdict aside and order a new trial at the close of a trial or on appeal is a convenient way of removing the consequences of error after it has occurred, of locking the door after the horse is stolen. But it does not prevent the error's happening, which ought to be the first concern of the judge in the trial of an action at law.

In New York there is no lack of power in the judge to comment on the evidence or even express an opinion upon it, if he follows the rule laid down by Judge Gray and leaves to the jury the decision of questions of fact. There is, however, a popular impression that judges in New York do not have this power, and in many cases a singular unwillingness to exercise it. Judge Gaynor, when sitting as a judge in the Appellate Division in the Second Department, referred to this unwillingness in characteristic manner, saying (Finnan *vs.* R. R. Co., 111 App. Div. 384):

"The appellant's fault-finding with the trial judge seems to be based on the notion that trial judges in this state are reduced to the humiliating position of having no right to say or do anything in a jury trial except to formally rule in monosyllables on questions presented by counsel; that they may do nothing to guide and control the course of the trial, or to restrain counsel and keep them within bounds and to the point, or even from taking an unfair advantage by prejudicing the jury by false suggestions, and the like. Horne Tooke told Lord Kenyon, before whom he was being sued, that his Lordship's only business was to help the tipstaffs keep order while the jury and counsel tried the case. But that extraordinary personage said it in good humor and altogether reprovingly, and to illustrate the independence of juries on questions of fact, and it was taken in that sense; while the serious and growing disposition of some in this state seems of late to be to actually reduce a trial judge to that position in the trial of civil causes, and leave counsel to do as they please. It would not be well for the administration of justice in this state if that purpose should prevail. When trial by judge and jury is reduced to trial by jury only, the uncertainties in the administration of justice will be increased tenfold. Trial judges in this State are under the law a light and a guide to juries. They may often appropriately even express their opinions on the facts to the jury in civil causes, provided they fairly leave the decision of the questions of fact to the jury, and frequently to do so."

Is it to be wondered at that in England, with its vast interests, with its chief city the financial and commercial center of the world, with its population of 40 millions of people, there are less appeals than in the state of New York with less than one-fourth of the number of the English population? Judge Gaynor undoubtedly stated the sound rule of judicial power over the conduct of trials in this state, and he also stated what unfortunately is true, that there is a growing disposition to reduce the judge to the position in which Horne Tooke tried unsuccessfully to place Lord Kenyon.

A very general cause of prolonged litigation with consequent delay in reaching its final determination is the statutory limitation on the powers of appellate courts to correct errors by a modification or reversal of the judgment from which an appeal is taken instead of sending the case back for a new trial. It often happens that some error upon the trial requires modification or reversal of the judgment and that upon the record of the case an appellate court can see that such is the proper disposition of it. But if the court is powerless to do anything but order a new trial, or if it has power and is unwilling to exercise it, it sends the parties back on their weary way to travel again the road of the new trial, the double appeal, perhaps only to be again sent back to repeat the experience. This was formerly necessary in New York, where, however, by statute, the powers of both the Appellate Division and the Court of Appeals have been increased so as to authorize the court on appeal to modify or reverse the judgment of the court below and enter judgment accordingly without a new trial. As, however, the Court of Appeals in many cases has no authority to review questions of fact, in all such cases the court is practically unable to exercise the power conferred upon it. A proposal now made and indorsed very generally by lawyers for consideration by the pending Constitutional Convention in New York is that a constitutional provision be adopted authorizing the Court of Appeals to review questions of fact in all cases appealed to it, and conferring on both the Court of Appeals and the Appellate Division power to award final judgment without new trial in all cases, if the court is satisfied that the record on appeal warrants such disposition. Such a provision would eliminate the necessity which now exists in a very large number of cases, of sending a case back for a new trial instead of the court's directing judgment in accordance with its view of the law and of the facts as shown by the record.

A typical, although perhaps extreme, example of the inconveniences which may arise where the appellate court is unable or unwilling to modify a judgment and direct entry of a final judgment accordingly, is *Williams* vs. *D. L. & W. R. R. Co.*, which was litigated in our own state. In this case a suit by a brakeman to recover damages for personal injuries was seven times tried before a jury. After the first two trials the Court of Appeals having held that on the plaintiff's own testimony the trial court should have directed a verdict against him, the plaintiff changed his testimony, and with the testimony thus changed at last secured a verdict and a judgment. The court commenting on the case said:

> "It frequently happens that cases appear and reappear in this court after three or four trials, where the plaintiff has changed his testimony in order to meet the varying fortunes of the case on appeal."[1]

Cases of this kind are, of course, extreme and exceptional. The possibility of them, however, should not exist, and they illustrate in striking fashion the consequences of a want of power in appellate judges or their unwillingness to exercise it in many states which, if it existed and were properly exercised, would have put an end to such an interminable round of trials, and appeals.

The disposition to minimize the power of the judge on the trial and on appeal, which has had such an unfortunate effect on the procedure of trials, is undoubtedly due to the popular distrust of judicial power which has manifested itself in this country in the adoption of the elective system and of various legislative enactments limiting the power of judges in particular ways. The dependence of the judge on popular approval in order to retain his office is a constant temptation to him to evade the responsibilities which are properly his, by placing them on the jury, and this has undoubtedly resulted in an unwillingness on the part of many elected judges to exercise the power conferred upon them.

The true remedy for the delays and disappointments of our present system does not lie in increasing the

[1] See "Treadmill Justice," by George W. Alger, *Atlantic Monthly*, Vol. 104, p. 696.

number of judges. In New York we have 109 Supreme Court and Court of Appeals judges, or approximately one judge to each 100,000 inhabitants — leaving out of consideration, of course, the County judges, the judges of the City Court and of the various inferior courts of the state. In England and Scotland there are judges exercising powers corresponding to those of our Supreme Court and Court of Appeals judges numbering 49, or approximately one judge for each 840,000 of the population. In other words, New York has more than eight times as many judges in proportion to its population as has England and Scotland. If we include in our computation the County judges in both countries, there are in England and Scotland 137 judges, or approximately one judge to each 300,000 population. In New York there are 186 judges, including the County judges, giving approximately one judge to each 57,000 of population.[1] By continuing to increase the number of judges, we can, of course, continue to do in increasing volume, in the way in which we are now doing it, a great deal of judicial business which ought not to be done at all. Lincoln's advice to lawyers, "Discourage litigation," may well be applied to the policy of a state. If, with a greater proportion of judges as compared with our population than England, our court calendars are still crowded, and there are still complaints about the law's delays, should we not begin to try the experiment of discouraging litigation by returning to the English system by improving the character of our Bar, by giving the judges greater power and responsibility in litigation and freeing them from the ever increasing burden of legislative codes?

[1] See note on page 225.

A burden cast upon judges and lawyers, and consequently upon the administration of law, in this country, which threatens to be overwhelming, is the steadily increasing volume of both written and unwritten law. In 1821, when all the law reports of the United States were comprised in 170 volumes, we find Judge Story lamenting the rapid increase in the mass of the law, and Kent, in his commentaries, spoke of the "multiplicity of law books" as "an evil that has become intolerable." The discussion of the project for codification of the common law which received great impetus at about this time was based in part on the assumption that the great volume of reports rendered codification inevitable. It is difficult to imagine what would have been the reflections of Story and Kent had they foreseen that the reports in the United States would reach in 1915 a total of something over 9000 volumes or that the lawyer of New York in 1915 would have in his library more than 940 volumes of reports in his own state and 453 volumes of reports of the Federal Courts, to say nothing of text-books, digests, and the reports of other states, and that he would add to his library in each year at the rate of 4 volumes of the reports of the Court of Appeals, 5 volumes of the reports of the Appellate Division, 5 volumes of the reports of inferior courts, 5 volumes of reports of the United States Supreme Çourts, 9 volumes of reports of the Federal Courts, or 28 volumes in all.

Senator Root has lately made a compilation of the law reports in this country, in which he finds that during five years ending December 1, 1913, the courts in this country rendered 65,000 decisions, in which opinions were written filling 630 published volumes.

In an earlier chapter I explained to you how the common law had grown and expanded as a law of precedent, and the significance of precedent in determining the law, and as an aid to judges and lawyers in administering the law. The multiplication of reports is indeed becoming an intolerable burden, not only to judges and lawyers in the first instance, but to litigants and ultimately to the public at large. No lawyer can now know or even refer to all the precedents on a given subject as could Story and Kent in their day. If he attempted to read all of the annual reports of the state and Federal courts, he would have little time left for the business of clients. Unless he knows well his legal landmarks, he will be in danger of becoming lost in a wilderness of reported decisions, often conflicting, sometimes overlooking previous decisions on the same subject and always progressively increasing in number.

This increase in volume of the law reports is, of course, due primarily to the vast increase in litigation, resulting in appeals to higher courts, whose opinions make the reports, but the real causes of their unwieldiness are the invention of stenography and typewriting, the multiplication of reports, digests, and legal literature of every type, with the consequent increase in size and elaborateness of lawyers' briefs, and finally the passion of the modern judge for exhausting his store of legal learning, and the time and patience of the reader at the same time, in each opinion which he writes. It is significant that the epoch-making decisions of the early common-law judges were models of brevity. The opinion of the court in Shelly's case, the famous case which decided that an heir took real estate by descent, occupies less than an ordinary page. The opinion in Spencer's case, which established the rule that the benefit of a covenant "touching and concerning land" passed to a transferee of the land, was less than two pages in length. The opinion in Slade's case, which established the right to recover damages for breach of special contract, was equally brief. Coming down to later times, the opinion of the House of Lords, in McNaghten's case in 1843, which established the modern rule relating to insanity as a defense for crime, occupies only four pages in the English reprint of the opinion. The opinions of Judge Shaw, many of them epoch-making in American legal history, were commonly two or three pages only in length, and they are notable for their clearness and accuracy. But to-day one may turn to volume after volume of the current reports and find decisions of no particular public interest, involving not a single new principle of law, which must needs be supported by elaborate opinions and copious citation of authorities. Principles relating to the law of contracts, or negligence, for example, which have been settled for at least fifty years, are constantly reiterated.

One may ask why write an opinion at all in cases which involve only questions of law, which are well settled, and thus add to the volume of legal literature material which is of no real value from the point of view of legal history and scholarship. A partial answer is, of course, that litigants and their counsel are entitled to know the reasons for the decisions of the court. There is no reason, however, why both would not be willing to have these reasons given in concise memorandum form, and it is quite possible to prepare the memorandum in such form that it would accomplish its purpose, without giving to it any value or influence as a precedent. Unless courts set some restraints on the length and number of published opinions, it is inevitable that our present system of making the law reports the chief repository of our unwritten law will break down of its own weight. The alternative is either a gradual loss in the weight and force of precedent, and the substitution of rules or principles of theoretical jurisprudence so far as they are commonly accepted by the courts, or codification. Either course would not be an unmixed evil. But that they are very generally regarded as evils by lawyers cannot be doubted, and that the time is not yet opportune for such radical changes in our law would, I think, be very generally conceded.

Still more formidable is the mass of legislative law enacted annually in this country. According to Senator Root, Congress and the legislatures of the states of this country passed during the four years ending December 1, 1913, more than 62,000 laws. During the last five annual sessions of the legislature of New York that body has passed 3583 laws, filling 11,110 printed pages. During substantially the same period, embodying a little more than the reign of the present king of England, the English Parliament passed only 256 public laws, aggregating 1602 printed pages. Last year the record of Parliament was 91 public laws, aggregating

483 pages, as contrasted with the work of our own legislature, which passed 582 laws, filling 2388 pages.

There is some difference in the legislative systems of the two countries to be taken into account, so that it is quite difficult to make an exact comparison between them; but it is substantially correct that the volume of legislation in New York is from three to four times as great as that of the English Parliament, although the population of New York is less than one-fourth as great as that directly affected by English legislation. And this is the result notwithstanding the vast interests of Great Britain and the fact that it is a great sovereign power exercising all the functions of government in its internal and external relations, whereas legislation in New York necessarily deals with only its internal affairs and with those functions of government retained by it under the Federal Constitution. To this overwhelming mass of legislation, poured out on the devoted heads of our people, may be attributed many of the existing evils of our legal system. It loads down our courts with litigation, it hampers them with a never ending succession of acts regulating and changing their organization, jurisdiction, and procedure.

What is perhaps even more serious, is that the practice of constantly adding new and changing old laws, many of which are never enforced, until the whole mass is beyond the powers of the human mind to grasp and comprehend, tends to bring all law into contempt, and to destroy the feeling of respect for law which must lie at the foundation of any adequate system of justice.

The evils of legislation in this country are due not

alone to its quantity, but to its quality. The drawing of a legislative act requires very exceptional training, experience, and skill. A man who attempted to alter or repair a delicate and complicated piece of machinery without the assistance of a trained engineer or mechanic, would be regarded as a species of lunatic; and yet we exhibit precisely this same kind of lunacy in the preparation of the great mass of our legislation. Practically no legislation can be enacted without affecting preëxisting law, written or unwritten, oftentimes both. The legislative draftsman, therefore, must know the exact legal situation which is to be affected by the proposed legislation, both historically and as a matter of existing law. He must know exactly the end to be accomplished and how it can be accomplished, without enacting into law provisions which repeal or do not harmonize with law intended to be preserved. This task requires wide knowledge and special training, and above all deliberation and painstaking effort, methods which are all too seldom employed in drafting legislative bills.

The result is that a very large proportion of the legislation of the country is crudely drawn. The language used is vague and technically inaccurate; words and phrases of uncertain meaning are often used instead of those which have been interpreted by courts or have acquired by long usage a definite legal significance. The history, interpretation, and practical operation of existing law are too often disregarded altogether. The result is that the courts and lawyers are left to struggle with this confused mass of ill-considered and undigested litigation at the expense of clients and of the general public welfare.

The reasons for this monumental folly are easily discerned. To some extent they lie in the popular belief, more highly developed in this country, I believe, than in any other, at the present time, that every ill that the flesh is heir to can be cured by legislative fiat; but mainly because of certain fundamental defects in our legislative system.

Any member of a legislature may introduce bills, without regard to their form or substance, and all members of legislatures usually introduce bills on request. The consequence is that the first week of the legislative session finds an enormous number of bills introduced and referred to committees. To select two examples that are typical, in 1913, 3922 bills were introduced into the California Legislature. In New York, between the opening date of the legislative session in January and the 25th day of March, 2928 bills were introduced. It is often quite beyond the powers of committees to do the work of considering and reviewing adequately this mass of proposed legislation. If the purposes of the bills seem good, it generally results that they are reported out and that the closing days of the legislative session are taken up with the wholesale passing of bills which have never been the subject of careful study by any legislative agency.

The small quantity and generally excellent quality of English legislation is explained very largely by the fact that under the English parliamentary system no bill can be introduced as a matter of right, but only on the leave of the legislative body, which means in the case of the House of Commons only on leave of the leaders of the party in power who thus acquire direct control over the form and substance of legislation. This system resulted in the permanent establishment in 1869 of the office of the Parliamentary Counsel, who, with an assistant and a clerical staff, does the work of drafting and revising all bills for public laws which are introduced into Parliament. There is thus a direct check on the amount of legislation, and through the expert aid of the Parliamentary Counsel and his permanent staff of assistants its quality is generally excellent and conforms to established legislative forms and practices.

In the past few years there has been a growing recognition of the necessity of improved legislative methods, which has borne fruit in the passage of acts in a number of states requiring all bills to be introduced in the early days of the legislative session, and for the establishment, in connection with the Library of Congress and in several of the states, of legislative reference bureaus or legislative drafting commissions. A legislative research fund has been established at Columbia University for similar purposes. Such organizations can render expert assistance in legislation when it is desired and availed of; but our legislative problem cannot be fully solved without some authoritative control over legislation corresponding to that of the English system, by which the volume of legislation at any session is checked, and all bills are required to be submitted to the scrutiny of the government draftsman.

No discussion of the subject of law reform should omit some reference to the subject of codification; that is, the enactment into more or less permanent legislative form of the rules and principles of the unwritten or common law. The notion of a legal code which should embody in precise written form all of the laws, so that he who runs may read, has always made its appeal to the idealist and the theorist.

The sentiment in favor of a general codification of our common law received its great impetus and reached its height in this country during the first half of the nineteenth century. Distrust of the common law as an English institution, naturally the subject of suspicion after the Revolution, the rapid increase in the number of law reports, the successful establishment of the Code Napoleon in France, all tended to prepare the public mind for the acceptance of the theories of Jeremy Bentham, the great English law reformer. Bentham, whose famous essays on law reform made their appearance and were widely read in this country from the revolutionary period to the time of his death in 1832, was the determined enemy of the common law and the most celebrated and persuasive advocate of universal codification. A code he defined as a "body of law, from the respective parts of which we may each of us, by reading them or hearing them read, learn and on each occasion know what are his rights and duties."

Bentham was an extremist, without comprehension of the practical difficulties, and in some respects the impossibility of carrying into effect his scheme of reform. He ignored the influences and teaching of history, disregarded the certainty of new and essentially changing conditions to which any system of law must be applied. His theory that by legislation there could be enacted a complete and comprehensive code of written law, by the aid of which every man could be his own lawyer, has long since been abandoned. The most loyal and enthusiastic advocates of codification now recognize that a code, to be effective, must be limited to a statement of general principles, and that the work of interpreting and applying it must be left to the judges and the lawyers. Nevertheless, Bentham's writings have had profound influence, and there are few law reforms in the past hundred years which are not directly traceable to them.

Perhaps the most notable effort at codification in this country is the justly celebrated code of Louisiana, prepared by Edward Livingston. Livingston, who was of the famous New York family of that name, settled in Louisiana in 1804, and under the direct influence of Bentham's writings prepared the Louisiana Code of Procedure, adopted by the legislature in 1805. In 1824, at the request of the Louisiana legislature, Livingston had prepared a code of laws relating to crimes, punishments, criminal procedure, and evidence. This was only partly adopted by the legislature, but the work of Livingston as a whole has been generally and rightly regarded as a great achievement, marking him as a great legislator, possessing those qualities of mind which are essential to successful codification, and which were wanting in Bentham, notwithstanding his great powers of inspiring interest in the subject of law reform.

This program for general codification of the common law was destined to failure, for the simple reason that the enormous difficulties involved in reducing the entire body of the common law to written form, which should at once be just and comprehensive, sufficiently precise and at the same time elastic enough to meet future needs, greatly outweighed the inconvenience and occasional injustices of the common-law system.

The history of the Code Napoleon, as well as that of lesser attempts at codification, teaches us that codification comes only when the inconveniences of an existing system are so great as to induce both lawyers and laymen to be willing to endure the burden of preparing a code and adjusting themselves to it.

More or less comprehensive codifications were prepared in Massachusetts under the leadership of Edward Everett; by Salmon P. Chase, in Ohio, and David Dudley Field in New York; all of which failed of adoption.

Codification on a more limited scale in the form of a revision of the statute law, including the codification of the real property law and the law of trusts, prepared by a commission headed by James Kent, was adopted in New York in 1828. This followed three less noteworthy attempts at revision between 1786 and that date. Similar revisions of statute law with code additions took place in Pennsylvania and Massachusetts in 1836.

The codification of the law of real property and the law of trusts in New York raised new questions for settlement by the courts. The codification of the law of trusts, especially, attempted in many particulars to wipe out the distinctions between legal and equitable interests, which were inherent in the nature of the subject, and it left out of account the teachings of the history of the subject. The result was that it required the decisions of courts and engaged the efforts of lawyers for at least one generation to answer these questions and to reduce the confusion produced by the codification to order and system. I think that on the whole the opinion of lawyers is that the benefits accruing from the codification of the law of trusts, for example, have just about been offset by the inconveniences and litigation which it has caused.

The movement for codification of procedure was inaugurated in New York in 1848 by the adoption of the Field Code, revised in substantially its present form in 1876. This code has been substantially copied in about one-half the states, with the results which were referred to at some length in the lecture on Procedure. A Short Practice Act was adopted in Massachusetts in 1851 and has been followed substantially in six states. Other states have continued with the common law procedure, more or less modified by statute.

A more recent and more commendable movement for codification had its origin in the creation of the Commission for Uniform State Laws, appointed in 1892. The commission consists of representatives of each of the states, appointed by the governor, who were called together for the purpose of drafting and recommending for adoption by the various legislatures forms of bills "to make uniform the law of the different states and territories on various subjects on which uniformity seems practicable and desirable." The commission has continued its labors down to the present day, and they have been attended on the whole by general success. The reasons for this success are threefold, and I dwell on them because they point the way to all successful law reform by way of legislation. They are:

First. The commission has been made up of lawyers who are very generally men of high character and professional standing and they have availed themselves freely of the advice and assistance of experts in the particular field in which legislation has been prepared.

Second. They have attempted to codify only a comparatively small part of the whole Common Law, in contrast to the more ambitious schemes of the early codifiers to reduce all law into a code.

Third. The particular portion of the law selected for codification has generally been that in which definiteness and certainty of the legal rule are more important than elasticity and adaptability to new conditions. This is particularly the case in the law of negotiable instruments and in the law of sales of goods.

The commission, since its organization twenty-four years ago, has now recommended eleven bills, including a Negotiable Instruments Act, a Warehouse Receipts Act, a Bill of Lading Act, a Sales Act, a Stock Transfer Act, and a Divorce Act, and others which need not now be mentioned. The Negotiable Instruments Act has been adopted in forty-three states, the Warehouse Receipts Act in twenty-eight, the Bill of Lading Act in eleven, the Sales Act in ten.

The history of the commission and the practical success of its work suggest the essential requirements of effective law reform. Law should be reformed by lawyers, for they have the knowledge, experience, and special training essential to the task of planning reforms and carrying them out, provided they are inspired with the sincere desire to correct the faults and abuses of an existing system.

In Bentham's time, lawyers were not inspired with any such desire, and it required the lash of his writings and his bitter attacks on law and lawyers to stir into activity the slumbering spirit of reform. To-day no such condition exists. The better element in the legal profession is not apathetic. The records of our various law organizations, the city, state, and national bar associations, show that there is an alert and healthy interest in the subject of law reform, and that it is none the less effective because intelligent and cautious. Our experience with codification has taught us that experiments in law reform must be cautiously made, with deliberation and painstaking study of the evil to be remedied, and the methods to be employed in remedying them, and, above all, all reforms should be inspired by the desire to correct real and substantial abuses and not merely to satisfy the aspirations of theorists and doctrinaires to bring about the millennium in law administration.

If, in my occasional critical references to some features of our legal system, I have given the impression of any want of faith or belief in our legal institutions, I desire to close by correcting that impression. As a lawyer and a citizen, I am proud of our legal institutions and have unwavering faith that their future will be even greater than their past. In our legal system lies the assurance of protection of our lives, liberty, property, and happiness, and that of our children and children's children. No more sacred duty rests on the lawyer and layman alike than that of defending, maintaining, and improving it.

Note

See page 210. Owing to differences in the organization of the two judicial systems, these statistics do not afford a basis for accurate comparison, but they do indicate the essential fact that we have a much greater number of judges in proportion to population than England, notwithstanding its greater business and financial interests.

INDEX